Standing on High Places

The Story of
Hannah Hurnard
and
Hinds' Feet on High Places

STANDING ON HIGH PLACES

ISABEL ANDERS

Tyndale House Publishers, Inc
Wheaton, Illinois

Cover illustration © 1992 Tim Jonke.
Photographs are from the private collections of Ruth Laurence and Marjorie Hurnard and are reprinted with their kind permission.

Excerpts from selected works and letters of Hannah Hurnard printed by permission of Tyndale House Publishers, Inc. and the Church's Ministry Among the Jews.
The poem "Travelers on the Road of Life" on p. xv is reprinted from Hannah Hurnard's memorial service brochure, November 3, 1990.

Unless otherwise indicated, Scripture quotations are taken from the *Holy Bible,* King James Version.

Scripture quotations marked NKJV are taken from The New King James Version. Copyright © 1979, 1980, 1982, Thomas Nelson, Inc., Publishers.

Scripture verses marked TLB are taken from *The Living Bible,* copyright © 1971 owned by assignment by KNT Charitable Trust. All rights reserved.

Library of Congress Cataloging-in-Publication Data

Anders, Isabel, date
   Standing on high places : the story of Hannah Hurnard and Hinds' feet on high places / Isabel Anders.
     p. cm.
   Includes bibliographical references.
   ISBN 0-8423-5933-8
   1. Hurnard, Hannah. 2. Missionaries—Israel—Biography. 3. Missionaries—Great Britain—Biography. 4. Missions to Jews—History—20th century. I. Title.
BV3202.H87A53   1994
209'.2—dc20
[B]   94-18881

Printed in the United States of America

00 99 98 97 96 95 94
10 9 8   7   6   5   4   3   2   1

For

Karen Winchell DuBert,

wayfarer for her Lord

in Mozambique

Contents

"Great Precipice Injury," from *Hinds' Feet on High Places*
"Last Scene on the Mountains of Spices," from *Mountains of Spices*
"Unity of Love," from *Kingdom of Love*
"The Wayfarer Leads Us Out," from *Wayfarer in the Land*
"The Wayfarer Teaches Us to Fish for Men," from *Wayfarer in the Land*
"God's Kingdom Is Here," from *Walking Among the Unseen*
"Love," from *God's Transmitters*
"Love in Oneness," from *Winged Life*
"Witness to a Miracle," from *Watchmen on the Walls*
"On the True High Places," from *Lessons Learned on the Slopes of the High Places*

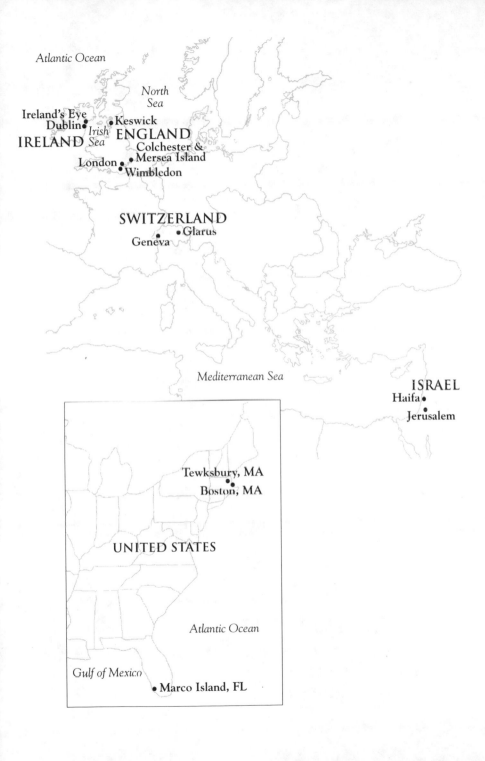

Foreword

Hannah Hurnard's name is held in much esteem among many people, not only for her magnificent ministry and wonderful writings, but also because of the sheer "fragrance" of her personality. She was a woman who walked with God.

I am immensely grateful for all she and Tyndale House Publishers have done for the mission Hannah loved and served so well for so many years.

"The Lord recompense thy work, and a full reward be given thee of the Lord God of Israel, under whose wings thou art come to trust" (Ruth 2:12).

The Rev. John Wood, MPhil, BD
Regional Adviser
Church's Ministry Among the Jews
"Shalom"
Colchester, Essex
England

Acknowledgments

I would like to express my gratefulness to Kenneth Petersen for his confidence in me, for giving me this book project, and for aiding and encouraging its development during the last three years.

I am thankful for the research and editing accomplished by Jill Rix every step of the way. I deeply appreciate her insights, her tirelessness, and her warm spirit of cooperation on this project. I also thank Kathy Stinnette for her editing insights and skills.

I wish to acknowledge also the encouragement and contribution of the Reverend John Wood, MPhil, BD, Regional Adviser of Church's Ministry Among the Jews in Colchester, Essex, England. His knowledge and help and his assistance in showing this manuscript to Marjorie Hurnard, Hannah's stepmother, for her review of its accuracy, are all greatly appreciated. He also kindly permitted his poem, which is at the end of the book, to be printed. And I thank Ruth Laurence and Susette Poole for their helpful contributions.

Last, but certainly not least, I thank my agent, Jane Jordan Browne, for all that she envisioned and accomplished. Her support has made all the difference.

Abbreviations

Extensive use of Hannah Hurnard's own writings has been made in preparing this biography. Where she is quoted directly, the source is identified by title or by one of the following abbreviations. Complete bibliographical information can be found at the end of the book.

HF   *Hinds' Feet on High Places*
HH   *Hearing Heart*
LL   *Lessons Learned on the Slopes of the High Places*
TSR   *Thou Shalt Remember*
WL   *Wayfarer in the Land*
WW   *Watchmen on the Walls*

Travelers on the Road of Life

Give us strength, O Lord we pray
    to travel on from day to day.
Along the path that leads until
    we reach full union with your will.

We've traveled far, but oh! we know
    we have a long, long way to go.
While there is pain, adversity
    throughout the world,
    we plainly see
Our work for you is far from done.
    Indeed, it hardly has begun.

Oh, make us channels as we go
    through which your healing love can flow.
To all the other souls around
    wherever pain and woe are found.

Blaze through us as a warm, clear light,
    solving Earth's problems—putting right
    its tragic wrongs.

This is our prayer:
    "Lord, in this glad work, let us share,
each moment hear your gentle call,
    to transmit your great love to all."

HANNAH HURNARD

Introduction

*Can you please let me know how I may get in touch with Hannah
Hurnard, the author of Hinds' Feet on High Places? . . . I must
tell her thank you for sharing her faith so beautifully, and how her
books have touched my life.*

Jill, Indiana

*Dear Hannah Hurnard: Our dear Heavenly Father has used you
to help and encourage me and many others with your words of
grace, glory, hope, peace and praise to him and to his only-begot-
ten Son, Jesus the Messiah. Hallelujah and Amen!*

Pat, California

These are samples of the many letters that have been written
to Hannah Hurnard.

Though she died in 1990, telephone queries and mail
addressed to her in care of her publishers still come from
readers who have been indelibly touched by her. They want
to know more about her writings, her personal background,
and her work in the British Isles, in Israel, and later in the
United States. They represent a network of faith—a connection of the Spirit.

Looking at her black and white portrait, one sees a
white-haired woman gazing strongly and steadily outward. In
this all-too-rare photograph, Hannah's face reflects a sense of
inner strength of purpose and persevering faith.

She had many interesting experiences and was blessed
with unusual insights throughout her fascinating life, and her
works reveal her unique testimony written along the way.

Hannah was an individual who dared to ask probing questions early in her life, such as, What would it be like to live on the heights of faith, service, and blessing?

In her unique, best-loved work, *Hinds' Feet on High Places*, she personally affirmed the declaration of the prophet Habakkuk: "The Lord God is my strength, and he will make my feet like hinds' feet, and he will make me to walk upon mine high places" (3:19; cf. 2 Sam. 22:34; Ps. 18:33).

I was privileged to meet Miss Hurnard in the early 1980s at the editorial office of her first United States publisher, Tyndale House. I had known of her and was familiar with her works since having read the British edition of *Hinds' Feet on High Places* almost twenty years earlier. During her visit to our offices, I was impressed with Hannah's humble appearance and manner. She did not seem to think of herself as "special" in any way or deserving of any undue attention. Yet it was clear that she stood firm in her own beliefs.

On that day Hannah graciously autographed a copy of her second allegory, *Mountains of Spices*, which Tyndale House had just brought out in a new edition. The inscription contained these words of challenge: "Always, the still higher! Hannah Hurnard."

Later, I was to discover that there were numerous struggles and changes that had occurred within her. Many of us have since learned about some of her personal opinions and emphases evidenced in her later writings and her public speaking engagements, and we have become concerned about what happened to her orthodox faith and her priorities.

Since this book is a spiritual biography, it necessarily addresses Hannah Hurnard's views as her life progressed. Readers are invited to consider the life journey of this remarkable woman, not as her judges or as her disciples, but as seekers and fellow servants of the Good Shepherd, who loves and cares for us all. In short, we will discover what one human life can show us of the life of service and of the pitfalls and sidetracks that any of us can stumble into at any time. Hannah Hurnard's life and its lessons can serve to make us even more mindful of our dependence on God to do God's work.

A closer examination of the perils and glories of such a spiritual walk has led me to write this story of Hannah Hurnard's life, faith, and legacy. Our starting place is a poem from the pen of this remarkable woman. It invites all sincere travelers to "the Heights," which are meant to be our everlasting home and habitat.

One

WILDERNESS WANDERINGS

But Moses pleaded, "O Lord, I'm just not a
good speaker. I never have been, and I'm not
now, even after you have spoken to me, for I
have a speech impediment."
"Who makes mouths?" Jehovah asked him.
"Isn't it I, the Lord? Who makes a man so that
he can speak or not speak, see or not see, hear
or not hear? Now go ahead and do as I tell you,
for I will help you to speak well, and I will tell
you what to say."

Exodus 4:10-12, TLB

U ntil I was nineteen years old, I never knew what it was like to feel happy," Hannah Hurnard once said. Yet early in her life, she had beheld a view of what "home" and "heaven" *could* be like. It was through nature, the beauty of Switzerland, especially, that she had caught a glint of what peace and love might mean. When she was four years old, and then again when she was six and eight, she was taken along by her parents, with a group of relatives and friends, to spend a few winter weeks in the Alps.

Much later, she would write of her feelings:

> The beauty of the snow and pine woods and the shining cloudless blue skies seemed to arouse in me the certainty that once, somewhere, I had known and experienced a condition of being in a realm of overwhelming beauty, safety, and happy companionship. . . .
>
> In that place there was no night nor any kind of darkness and no gaping holes in the earth into which

3

bodies were put and covered over and left forever. How my heart ached with longing to find my way back into the vanished world of peace and joy! (TSR)

These were her first glimpses of the "High Places" that would someday inspire her greatest life's work, *Hinds' Feet on High Places*. Even as a child, Hannah was "afflicted with transcendence"—marked with a longing for heaven. Her openness to wherever that might lead was to bring her naturally to the place of sacrifice: a life of service.

Her grandfather James Hurnard was Colchester's most prodigious poet. Though he never made much money selling his work, he received a considerable inheritance soon after his son, Samuel (Hannah's father), was born, which enabled his family to live very well. Hannah's father inherited the family fortune, so his family, too, was comfortably provided for. Seven servants ran their well-equipped ten-bedroom house, "Hill House," in Colchester, Essex. Four of these staff were either nurses or nannies to the four Hurnard children, which included an older sister, Ruth, an older brother, Bracy, Hannah, and a younger sister, Naomi. Yet, despite this inherited wealth and prosperity, there was something lacking in Hannah's life. A deeply sensitive young girl, she preferred the company of her exotic pet birds and the peaceful glories of nature to that of other people.

Her mother, Rose Hurnard (nee Densham), had been born to an aristocratic English family living on the Isle of Wight, who were on a first name basis with royalty. Rose was often ill but kept herself occupied with altruistic work during most of her periods of health. She preached, taught, and also ministered charitably to soldiers. Despite her poor health, her mother was always, in Hannah's words, a "joyful lover of the Lord."

Each Sunday Hannah, as a small girl, and her family, plus their pet dog, would walk two miles or more to the Railway Mission in Colchester for morning worship. Then in the evening, they would attend a mission service in the Lexden Village Hall, which her grandmother had had built.

Because it was the custom of well-to-do families in the first decade of the twentieth century, the Hurnards agreed to send Hannah to boarding school at age seven. They hoped it would help her improve her social skills and further her education—a privilege for a young girl of that time. But Hannah was an outcast among her young peers.

For Hannah had a speech impediment, and of the most seemingly hopeless kind. She later wrote, "I developed a distressing stutter and was often unable to do anything but grimace, make ugly sounds, and dribble and even spit" (TSR). Contact with other children in the school yard was a nightmare to her. She did not easily make friends, since her stammering tongue and many anxieties about life kept her isolated and in a dark room of self for many years. At school, right in front of gaping bystanders, Hannah would sometimes have what seemed to be uncontrollable seizures: falling headlong to the ground, shrieking, and shaking in frustration.

Hannah always remembered her early childhood days with anxiety and shame because a nervous breakdown over her speech and personal problems had sent her home from boarding school in disgrace. It was hardly the way a rich girl was supposed to behave or present herself, especially in the Victorian-influenced English society of her day. Thereafter, she was tutored at home. It was embarrassing and humiliating to be Hannah Hurnard.

Hannah's playmates consisted of her siblings and children of other wealthy families who visited her home or whose homes she visited. Rarely comfortable in social situations, she always felt like a misfit in the company of other children her age, mostly because of her verbal handicap.

As Quakers, the Hurnards stressed the guidance of the Holy Spirit, often referred to as "the inner light" of God's presence. The children were expected to sit silently for hours at Friends meetings, where worshipful silence invited God to speak to individual hearts. For Hannah this was torturous, as she could not seem to make contact with the God she was supposed to know, love, and serve. It was not that she hadn't *tried* to experience God's peace and a love for God's Word, as the rest of her family did, and to grow in the spiritual life they so valued. Her parents' example and Puritan teaching had helped lead their daughter to believe in the existence of God and to give herself to the unseen Savior at eleven years of age. Even so, she had a hard time feeling close to God. "I prayed," she would later write, "but there was no answer. I went to gospel services, and was unutterably bored and depressed. I repented, but I couldn't stop doing wrong things. I read the Bible and found it the dullest and most lifeless book in the world" (HH).

Feeling far from God was not *just* "something missing" in her life. It was a gaping hole—a state of torment in which she lived daily, much like the Jews while in bondage to the Egyptians. Constantly during these early years, she felt lonely, afflicted, and despairing.

But then in July 1924 her whole life changed.

Two

THE CALL
TO
HIGH
PLACES

The Lord so loves to give to us
His radiant, perfect peace.
The world cannot take it away
And it will never cease.

If you'll believe this and will live
As though our Lord you saw,
You'll find that He is with you still
But closer than before!

"In Heavenly Places" live with Him,
In realms of highest power,
Where He in you and you in Him
Can live each day and hour

With power to do still greater works.
And you'll His body be,
Through which He daily carries on
His saving ministry.

Hannah Hurnard, in a letter dated March 5, 1989

I n the summer of 1924, Hannah's father announced that he wanted her to accompany him to the annual Keswick Convention, a summer conference and gathering of evangelical Christians from all over the British Isles. Hannah was horrified at the very thought of having to go to religious meetings all day long, shut up with a crowd of people in a tent, and at first she refused. But finally they made a bargain together. Hannah would go with him to the convention, attending one meeting each morning and one each evening—then the rest of the day she would be free to wander out on the hills of rolling Cumberland, a county in northwest England.

The Keswick Convention was held in the Lake District of England, which also was the home province of the great Romantic poets—most notably, Wordsworth. In this beautiful place, where sheep roam freely, crags and three-thousand-foot-high mountains ring blue lakes like "jewels around the Queen's neck."

Enjoyment of the terrain of her native England had always been one of Hannah's few joys. She loved the freedom that she found in nature and wrote of its beauty in this passage from *Hinds' Feet:*

> A long-deferred spring was just loosening everything from the grip of winter, and all the trees were bursting into fairest green and the buds were swelling. In between the trees were glades of bluebells and wild anemones, and violets and primroses grew in clumps along the mossy banks. Birds sang and called to one another and rustled about, busily absorbed in nest-building.

Could Hannah dare to hope for a springtime in her heart as well? In the depths of her soul she reasoned: *If there really is a God, surely the Keswick Convention is the place where he is most likely to reveal himself to me. And if I don't find him, it will be complete confirmation that the whole thing is wishful thinking or delusion.*

And I will keep my word to Father, she determined as she went through the whole week of the convention, attending two meetings a day in the great tent. Above fluttered pennants spelling out *Love, Joy,* and *Hope.* Hanging over the speaker's platform inside were the words All One in Christ

Jesus. Preachers of many denominations came to speak in turn, admonishing attendees to accept God's call to the "higher life."

It seemed that nothing spoke directly to Hannah that week. God was as unreal and unrevealed at the end of the week as he had ever been. The only result was that every day she seemed to grow more and more miserable. She was surrounded by thousands of people who all appeared to be happy and entirely sure of God—yet not a single speaker uttered a word that seemed to meet her need.

The convention ended on Friday, and the next morning a meeting of gathered missionaries was held. Inexplicably, Hannah chose not only to attend, but to sit in a crowded tent for the entire three hours of the session! Twelve missionaries, both men and women, got up one by one and not only *spoke*, but *shone* with the light of God's presence.

It must be true. There must be a God, after all, who is able to save and transform even the most wretched and tormented—able and willing, apparently, to save everybody but me. Why can't I find him? Hannah desperately wondered.

The missionaries said their last words and sat down. Then the chairman of the meeting rose and extended an "altar call" to young men and women who were ready and willing to respond to God's challenge to serve on the mission field. Hannah intuitively knew the high stakes that were involved.

While she was still in her mother's womb, her parents had dedicated her to be a missionary. "They had told me so," she later wrote, "and I had almost hated them for so doing! With my stammering mouth, terror of human beings, and a fearful nature, I longed only to be able to stay sheltered all my life in a safe home surrounded by love and kindness and tender care. How could the idea of wanting anyone (least of all *me*) to spend his or her life as a missionary amid the dangers, discomforts, and persecutions in distant lands, have originated? It was the most frightful of all prospects that I could imagine!" (TSR).

Amid rustling sounds of movement, whisperings, and tears heard throughout the tent, many young people—perhaps hundreds—rose to signify their commitment to just such a life. Then, the chairman asked if there were any persons there who were willing to send *their children* to the field, if God so called them. To Hannah's horror, her own father stood in his place beside her, thus tightening the grip that was encasing her soul and heightening her sense of being trapped.

This was too much for Hannah. She sprang up from her seat and rushed from the tent, not out of claustrophobia, but from a much more penetrating fear. It was her blackest moment of all—the midnight hour in disoriented space with no point of a compass to guide her.

Perhaps out of habit, fear, or even defiance, she then found herself kneeling by her own bed in her cottage room. There she earnestly cried out: "O God, if you are there you must make yourself real to me. If you exist and are really what these people describe you to be, you can't leave me like this. If you don't reveal yourself I shall know that there is no hope anywhere in the universe, nothing but fear and loneliness and death and the utterly terrible unknown beyond that!"

Hannah grabbed her Bible and challenged God to speak to her through his Word. She opened the flapping pages haphazardly and saw that they had fallen to reveal 1 Kings

18. Horror filled her heart. "There you are! That's the sort of God you are. As if anything in this book of Kings with all their names and evil doings could possibly reveal a God of love."

She was about to close the book unread when she decided to give God one more chance. She dared to look at what was on the page. There she read the familiar passage of Elijah challenging the false prophets of Baal to call down fire from heaven to prove that their god really existed and would respond to their requests. As they prayed to Baal from Mt. Carmel, "there was neither voice, nor any to answer, nor any that regarded" (v. 29).

The young woman was stunned by the manner in which this Old Testament account described her own experience of asking for a sign of God's presence for so many years. The rest of the chapter completed the story and affected Hannah in an unexpected way. She read how Elijah repaired the altar of the Lord that had been broken down (v. 30) and laid upon that altar a sacrifice (v. 33). The prophet then said, "Hear me, O Lord, hear me, that this people may know that thou art the Lord God, and that thou hast turned their heart back again" (v. 37).

So this was it. The altar. The place of sacrifice. A thrill of terror went through her, with a pang of agony. Yes, here it was—the thing she had always dreaded. Before God revealed himself, he demanded a sacrifice. Christians said that Christ himself was the sacrifice, the substitute for *our* sacrifice. But in that bitter moment, she knew that there was no escape from the truth. "I, too, like those of old, must lay on the altar a sacrifice," Hannah concluded.

Just as clearly, Hannah saw what her sacrifice must be.

What this unknown God is going to demand before he makes himself real is that I yield to him my stammering tongue and agree to be his witness and messenger. Verse 21 also struck her to the heart: "How long halt ye between two opinions? if the Lord be God, follow him."

Hannah's life rushed before her. She saw herself, in her imagination, opening and shutting her mouth with a sea of embarrassed faces staring at her as she failed to be able to produce more than a tortured grunt or a stuttering cry.

"No, I can't do it," she wailed. "I would rather go straight to hell . . . but it's as though I am in hell already. . . ."

Why halt ye . . . how long halt ye? . . . Follow him . . . the Spirit urged.

"Oh, I need him. No one else can help me. . . ."

She continued praying in agony on her knees, until at last she heard herself surrender: "If you will make yourself real to me and help me, I *will* give you my stammering tongue, and I *will* become a missionary."

When she glanced over again at the open Bible on the bed, she saw in the passage in 1 Kings that "all the people . . . fell on their faces: and they said, The Lord, he is the God; the Lord, he is the God" (v. 39). At that moment, it was as though an ironbound door in her heart and mind was suddenly unlocked and flung open, and *light*—warm, glorious, and radiant—engulfed her as in a sea of love.

The impossible had happened.

As Hannah would later describe this pivotal moment: "Two loving arms went around me and a tender voice said gently, 'Here I am, Hannah. I have been here all the time, but you locked yourself away from the consciousness of me and my presence by refusing to yield yourself completely.

14

Now the block is gone and you know that I am here. I love you and I will never leave you. You will never be alone again."

Yet Hannah asked for another sign. "O God, if you love me and are real as you seem to be now in such a wonderful way, please confirm this experience so that I will never doubt it nor think it has been my imagination . . . please speak to me again as I open the Bible at some other page."

She quickly reopened her Bible, and the pages fell open to what was to become her life verse: "And he said unto me, My grace is sufficient for thee: for my strength is made perfect in weakness" (2 Cor. 12:9). Her parents had always told her that her name, *Hannah*, meant "God's grace"! This second assurance meant to her that whenever anyone would call her by name, she would immediately be reminded of these words and know, again, that in her own human weakness, God's grace would at last find its home.

The rest of verse 9 could hardly have been more assuring. She read it in wonder: "Most gladly therefore will I rather glory in my infirmities, that the power of Christ may rest upon me."

Outwardly everything was exactly the same. Her fearful nature was still there. Her dread of people was still there— and so was her complete ignorance of how to begin thinking about others and considering their interests. "I was still the old Hannah," she would later write, "but in some miraculous and mysterious way I had been lifted . . . out of the border land of outer darkness, into the light and glory of heaven. It was as though a miserable, stunted plant had suddenly been transplanted from a tiny flowerpot, into a sunny, richly fertilized flower bed. I was lifted out of the dreadful isolation

of self-imprisonment and set down in the love of God"
(HH).

At age nineteen, Hannah's life pilgrimage had truly
started to take shape.

Three

"MY GRACE IS SUFFICIENT"

*For Jehovah God is our Light and our Protec-
tor. He gives us grace and glory. No good thing
will he withhold from those who walk along his
paths.*

Psalm 84:11, TLB

*Thou comest to me with a sword, and with a
spear, and with a shield: but I come to thee in
the name of the Lord of hosts, the God of the
armies of Israel, whom thou hast defied.*

1 Samuel 17:45

Waking up to a cheerful chorus of birdsong and the
half-light of early morning, Hannah felt embraced by
peace. Turning slightly, she glanced over at her open Bible
next to the bed and pondered in amazement what had
transpired within her soul in so short a time. With a youthful,
energetic movement and the strength of a joy that could not
be suppressed, she leaped from her bed to begin her first full
day of *knowing* that *she* was a child of God.

No longer was it a secondhand knowledge passed down
from her parents. Now it was her own. "Thank you, Lord,"
she breathed, as she dressed and set out eagerly to attend a
Sunday worship service at one of the chapels in town.

Before those gathered in the small room stood a plainly
dressed woman, ready to address them. Hannah could not
help but notice the personal strength this woman conveyed
and the light of assurance in her eyes. She was Mrs. Booth
Clibborn, a leader in the Salvation Army, an evangelical

parachurch organization begun by her parents, William and Catherine Booth, in 1865.

This speaker had Hannah's rapt attention as soon as she began her presentation. After a few preliminaries, Mrs. Clibborn moved dramatically into painting a biblical scene. The subject of her message was the Old Testament passage about the boy David being sent to fight the formidable giant Goliath on the battlefield. Since Hannah was already familiar with this text, her active imagination was set afire.

Although Hannah was a young woman untrained for service, as she inwardly acknowledged, she anticipated *what God could do through a willing servant*. In her heart Hannah knew that she, too, was a warrior. And soon there would be "giants" in her way. She thought of how young David must have felt in the face of his mighty, towering opponent: small, afraid, and hopelessly outclassed. Her heart skipped a beat at the thought.

Then she remembered the victory that had already been won and felt herself drawing upon the strength of the past few hours of her bedside struggle. Her faith was genuine. But suddenly, her human weaknesses were plainly obvious to her as well. Hannah would later reflect, "Surely no pilgrim ever set out to follow the Lord with a more trembling and fearful heart than I did. Looking shrinkingly towards the future, it seemed to me that, handicapped as I was, every step of the way before me must cost pain and tears and humiliation . . ." (HH).

She thought again of David. *He was the youngest son of Jesse, a peaceful shepherd in a family of older brothers who were mightier warriors. Yet he was the one chosen to do battle with an enemy who was threatening to destroy all of Israel!* Seated in the crowded chapel, Hannah leaned forward and smoothed her dress over her knees. She settled her Bible in her lap, read along, and listened as intently as any recruit in training for battle would—straining her ears to catch all of the words.

Mrs. Clibborn retold the account of the boy who faced the giant, bearing only five small pebbles fished from a brook. These stones were, to her, the "simple promises of God," which Hannah sincerely wished to become armed with as well. As Hannah heard again the familiar words of how the unlikely youth was able to slay his enemy at the first blow, a flood of hope and encouragement swept into her very heart.

The preacher's next words seemed directly aimed at Hannah in her new state of commitment and readiness. "You, too," she intoned, seeming to point her long, slender finger straight at Hannah, "are afraid of some giant in the way before you. Never fear. Meet him in the name and strength of the God of David, and though you feel like a grasshopper in comparison with him, he will fall to the ground before you."

This was the special-delivery message Hannah took with her as she was preparing to leave Keswick. In the light of her newfound courage, she began to recall the other teachings she had heard at the convention *before* her heart had been moved. Suddenly, these principles of vital Christian growth began to take shape for her in a new way; those "pebbles" of strength were there to take her to the next step of her pilgrimage of faith.

They included, first, a warning to separate *from everything* that would tend to draw her back into the old life of unbelief. How important this was for one who had taken only a day's journey so far from her former skepticism and misery. Time

21

would reveal to her those special dangers and how she must avoid them on this path of obedience.

The second pebble was that they were urged to *begin witnessing* of their faith to others. "For if we were not willing to share in this way, we would soon find that we had nothing left to share," Hannah later recalled being taught. She began experiencing the important realization that to give what we have to others does not deplete us, for God refills us as he once kept an Old Testament widow's pot of oil full to the brim.

A third pebble was the reminder of *her own powerlessness*. Another of her teachers at Keswick was a Miss Bradshawe, a missionary from South India who served with Amy Carmichael, a well-known missionary, writer, and poet who died in 1951. She had explained the concept of dependence on God to Hannah and the others through the use of four white cardboard squares she held before them. They read:

I CAN'T.
CAN GOD?
GOD CAN.
I CAN do all things through Christ who strengthens me.

Hannah's fourth pebble promise had come to her as a ray of hope and would later shine into her heart to reach her through any darkness. One day, as Hannah had sat alone on a hillside during a break in conference meetings, she had watched while dark clouds began to glide across the sky. Suddenly, a shimmering rainbow appeared. Its two ends seemed to touch the ground on either side of her. Immediately, she accepted this as a sign and a reminder of God's covenant promise to Abraham: *I will be with you always . . . no matter the appearance or the circumstances. There is nothing to fear.* This, too, was a gift—of God's *strength and presence*.

Nonetheless, there was a fifth pebble that required something definite of Hannah from the very start of her journey of faith. It was the necessity of *a consistent quiet time* before God. Clarence Foster and the other Keswick leaders had called this "the morning watch." That was an appropriate battle term for God's servants who were striving to serve in the tradition of David and the prophets. They had been urged to rise at least three-quarters of an hour earlier every morning in order to meet the Lord and listen to him. This very simple but all-important act of obedience was to set the keynote for Hannah's life from that day on.

Mr. Foster, a kindly man whose face mirrored his concern, had spoken to the young people attending the conference in a language that was especially to take root and grow in young Hannah's mind and heart. "Will you not look on your Lord as the great Lover, and go to meet him in the same spirit?" He pointed out how natural and easy it is for lovers to agree to meet and to keep their "tryst" out of desire for each other's company. Hannah was to use this language and understanding of her relationship with the Lord in her writings. She would consistently invite others to "taste" this communion—this speaking heart to heart with the Savior—that was so vital a part of her own experience.

At one point in her young adulthood, Hannah fell in love with a young man. Looking forward to the opportunity to express human love with a life partner, Hannah desired to marry him. In *Hinds' Feet on High Places*, Miss Much-Afraid speaks to the Shepherd about her "great longing to experience the joy of natural, human love, and to learn to love supremely one person who will love me in return." Ultimately, however, the young man chose someone else to be his wife. Despite bitter disappointment over her loss, Hannah showed great strength. She was able to give her grief to God, deciding from that point on that the love of her Lord would be sufficient for her for the rest of her life. These words of Scripture comforted her: "For your Maker is your husband, The Lord of hosts is His name" (Isa. 54:5, NKJV). The man Hannah loved actually married a friend of hers. Much to her credit, Hannah continued to relate to this couple through the years, bearing whatever disappointment she felt within, with no outward signs of bitterness.

We can see in her writings poignant evidence of the power of this lost potential for romantic love. Its energy began to flow naturally through another channel—that of encouragement to other believers in their Christian walk. There are multitudes of passages in Hannah's works that beautifully express her deep sensibilities and her unique capacities for love and devotion, which were thereafter turned directly toward God. The "romantic" character of this love is best illustrated in the personal call of the Chief Shepherd (an allegorical picture of her Lord) in this passage from *Hinds' Feet*:

> You must be ready to follow me whenever I come to the cottage and call. I will give you a secret sign. I shall sing one of the Shepherd's songs as I pass . . . and it will contain a special message for you. When you hear it, come at once and follow me to the trysting place.

For young Hannah, all nature gleamed and spoke to her as God's bountiful creation. Such is the setting for her stories about the land of the Shepherd. Added to her skills of observation and phrases descriptive of nature, we find many accurate echoes of the language of Scripture itself. For it was in her daily reading and prayer time that she would always find that "secret sign" to call her to the trysting place with her Lord. That place was never very far from the altar of commitment. Thus, in the circumstances of her life in the out-of-doors, where she felt the most freedom, and in reading in the pages of the Bible, Hannah repeatedly encountered the Shepherd's unmistakable call, "Follow me."

Her relationship with Christ began to develop and, eventually, to deepen and mature. At Keswick, Clarence Foster had urged the young people to "look upon the Bible as his love letter, and read it over and over again with the joy and attention with which you read your earthly lover's letters" (HH). This sensitive, intelligent young adult took the words to heart as perhaps did no other person present in those meetings. The proof of this is the fruit of her work on the Christian mission field over a period of a lifetime. The second evidence, of course, is the way in which she was able to turn the beauty of those "love letters" (the biblical language of God's love) into enduring literature of spirituality. A number of these books continue to nourish the quiet times or the "morning watches" of thousands, perhaps millions, of people today worldwide.

Hannah was about to step into the adult world as a committed student and missionary candidate, while carrying with her two seemingly contradictory traits. These would greatly benefit her early career as well as distinguish her writings in later years. On the one hand, she had the *sincerity and dedication* of a new convert. On the other, she was blessed

25

with the *knowledge and depth* of a person steeped in Scripture. Best of all, being well acquainted with human imperfections through her handicaps and former fears, she was able to bring the healing balm of God's Word to the hearts of others who suffered in unbelief. Did she not know how God could touch her own mouth, her feet, her fears, and turn her deficits into assets? Though her journey to the "high places" was just beginning, she already had the marks of a leader, the single-mindedness, the determination, and the humility of a "hearing heart" that sustain her for the tasks ahead.

Hannah knew, as did the main character of *Hinds' Feet*, Miss Much-Afraid, that the first step is to hear the Shepherd's call; then, simply, to follow. *"As close behind the hart, there leaps the roe, So where thou goest, I will surely go."* That she did by learning to rise early every morning and go out to the quiet woods or by the shores of a glassy lake with her Bible and notebook in hand. There, she would begin studying, searching out promises, and finding her heart opening like a flower to the grace mediated through this intimate fellowship with her Lord.

She later wrote of that time, "As I turned to the Bible and read it again, it seemed as though my thoughts in some way received new illumination, my thinking became clearer, my understanding deeper than before. He used my ordinary mental faculties and encouraged me to ask questions all the time" (HH).

Admittedly, it was a struggle to wrench herself out of a comfortable bed each day to face such a discipline. Nonetheless, in this diligent attention to her inner life, she found the strength to move ahead with her plans to become a missionary. She knew instinctively that everything depended on this act of faithfulness to the light she had already received.

Hannah also began to exercise her faith in public despite her fears. In her own words, she was "beginning to confess with my stammering tongue to my acquaintances that I now believed in him . . . attempting to go into shops alone and on buses . . . beginning to do things for myself" (HH). As she did, she found both the strength for each necessary task and the assurance that she was indeed "on the way" as a follower of her Shepherd.

It is not surprising that the well-read Hannah chose the name of John Bunyan's character in *Pilgrim's Progress* Much-Afraid as the inspiration and title character for her own stories. She once wrote that, up to the time of her conversion, "the name which had best described my nature" was Bunyan's character Miss Much-Afraid. She later wrote in *Hearing Heart* that the Lord transformed and renamed her *as truly herself*: "He made my own name Hannah, which is the Hebrew word for Grace, my real, true name." As the Shepherd warns in *Hinds' Feet*: "Growing into the likeness of a new name is a long process." Hannah had begun that lifetime journey toward grace and glory.

About two and a half months after her conversion experience in 1924, she prepared to leave her father's home to go to Ridgelands Bible College of Wimbledon, Great Britain. There she would begin the process of being readied for missionary service. Surely, to this novice young believer, personal "giants" would come in the form of barriers that would threaten the fulfillment of her heart-promise to go to the mission field. But it was as "Hannah," and through the promises of God's provision, that she took the next decisive step.

Four

FRUIT OF
THE SPIRIT

But the fruit of the Spirit is love, joy, peace,
longsuffering, gentleness, goodness, faith,
meekness, temperance.

Galatians 5:22-23

As she stood on the mossy bank by the pool she
happened to glance down and noticed for the
first time that her feet were no longer the
crooked, ugly things which they always had
been, but were "straight feet," perfectly
formed, shining white against the soft green
grass.

from **Hinds' Feet on High Places**

R idgelands Bible College was located in Wimbledon, about sixty-five miles from Hannah's home in Colchester. In 1924, when Hannah set out, the journey involved a two-hour ride by steam train to London and then a long subway ride to Wimbledon—in total about a three- or four-hour ordeal.

Being trapped in a tiny compartment, watching unfamiliar scenes and people pass quickly by: that was what came to her mind at the mention of having to ride alone on a train or the city's underground transportation. It caused Hannah to shudder. She was bitterly certain that she would never be able to utter the name *Wimbledon* at the ticket office, nor *Ridgelands* to the taxi driver, as *W* and *R* were especially difficult sounds for her to pronounce.

However, in these small challenges, as well as in larger

ones, Hannah found her Shepherd faithful. Each time, the words she dreaded saying slid out surprisingly smoothly, but only as they were called for. Upon entering the college, she found that people were not so threatening, but rather helpful in showing her her room and even anticipating her needs. The Christian fellowship that she would discover, and the kindness of the people of this community, were to give her exactly the environment she needed in which to grow. On the other hand, its challenges were to test to the limit God's earlier promise to her that "my grace is sufficient."

To her distress, from the first days of college Hannah had one personal nightmare that just wouldn't go away. It was the speaker's class that all the students were compelled to attend every Thursday morning. Ridgeland's principal would first deliver a lecture offering hints and instructions for speakers—a practical approach for missionary candidates—then the students would take turns delivering short addresses.

The student speeches were followed by a feedback session in which the listeners would offer criticism, suggestions, and evaluations of the speaker's performance. This was not always a pleasant experience, even for gifted speakers in the class, and for Hannah it was a trial by fire. For a person who was totally inexperienced in such public speaking and who habitually stammered, it was an appalling prospect to stand before her peers and be judged wanting—at the very earliest stages of her professional training for service. Unhappily, Hannah learned that she was scheduled for the second or third week! That would leave little time for prayerful preparation. "Afterwards, of course," she later wrote, "I realized that this was all in the loving ordering of my Lord, for it would have been unbearable to have the ordeal hanging over me all the term" (HH).

On the Monday morning of the week she was scheduled to speak, Hannah awoke in fear, as she had so often in her childhood. Sweat collected on her forehead, and her hands shook nervously. She tried opening and closing her mouth, but it seemed disconnected from the rest of her. Surely she would be unable to perform under such duress, she worried.

Each time she thought about it, she cringed. *Maybe I should grab a ticket for home and simply leave this place fast.* Yet even as she considered fleeing in fear, the Lord's guidance gently came to her heart.

You can't do it, of course, Hannah. But isn't this just what you promised me you would attempt to do for my sake? Won't you trust me in this matter? Won't you put me to the test and see whether I fail you or not?

Her only answer was, "Yes, Lord." But even as she submitted to the seemingly impossible, she wept in terror.

When the dreaded Thursday morning arrived, Hannah found herself feeling physically ill at the prospect of facing the class to speak. Reluctantly, she dressed, breathed what seemed a shallow, ineffective prayer, and steeled herself for the coming ordeal. Irrational thoughts loomed like giants in her path, even the idea that she might drop dead of a heart attack or fright. Deliberately forcing aside these thoughts, she took her place among the other students as usual.

Following the principal's lecture, she was the *first* of the four students to be called to the front of the classroom to speak. Slowly Hannah got up out of her seat. Walking to the platform seemed like sailing off into the deep as a lonely vessel in total darkness. God seemed as remote as he ever had been in her early life. She took one step after another—by faith—until she reached the podium. Then, before the sea of expectant faces, an absolute miracle occurred! Totally and simply, her fear left her, and her words began to flow. She opened her mouth, and for the first time in her life found herself speaking *without a trace of stammer* or even hesitation, talking just like everyone else.

Always a diligent student, Hannah had prepared well. Her work, in sync with God's grace in the moment, brought a response of smiles and encouragement from her peers. When the class was over, one of the tutors came over to her and said, "Hannah, I am sure God has given you a gift for speaking. Consecrate it to him and determine never to say no when you are asked to speak at meetings for his glory." In that moment, she decided that her newfound voice, with its flow of unimpeded speech, would be God's alone. She would never use it for any other sort of public lecturing, but only for witnessing to his power.

Hannah touched her mouth in utter amazement. What had seemed so stiff, unresponsive, and paralyzed during her earlier anxiety attack, now was free, flexible, and, she knew, *made useful to God*. From that time on, Hannah's stammer—for all practical purposes—disappeared. Though sometimes a shadow of slurred speech crept into her ordinary conversations, especially when she was under stress, her preaching voice was clear and totally functional. She was discovering herself to be, indeed, a fit vessel for the work she had been called to do.

In *Hinds' Feet*, the scene in which Much-Afraid finds healing from her crippled feet sheds some light on this actual victory in Hannah's life. She writes of Much-Afraid: "She

34

felt completely encompassed by peace, and a great inner quietness and contentment drowned every feeling of curiosity, loneliness and anticipation. She did not think about the future at all. It was enough to . . . rest and recover herself after the long journey."

There was little time for Hannah to rest once she began her important work of sharing the words and works of Jesus Christ with others. Armed with the Authorized (King James) Version of the Bible, she visited house after house in seedy London slums. Besides that, she found herself speaking in starkly furnished gospel halls, at a temporary medical mission, and even during simple lunchtime meetings in factories. She actively preached the gospel "in season and out of season." Humbly and bravely, she seized every opportunity she had to talk, including her visits to the sick. In Wimbledon Common, she would even stand on a makeshift "soapbox" to witness to the remarkable deliverance she had experienced. In simplicity of speech, yet backed with much prayer, she offered to others the chance to begin their own journey with her Shepherd.

It was about this time that Hannah was phoned to come home, as her mother was dying. She arrived only a few days before her mother's passing. There was, during that visit, a touching of the hearts of mother and daughter such as they had never experienced before.

Rose Densham Hurnard had been raised in England as a Quaker. Often, while attending church with her husband and children, she felt moved by the Holy Spirit during the "meditation" periods to speak spiritual admonitions. Her gifts had been recognized, and she had been granted the right to preach and minister freely. During Hannah's teen years,

Mrs. Hurnard had suffered so much from debilitating weakness that she had to give up nearly all of her own evangelistic work. Yet when she refused speaking and preaching requests, she would inevitably predict in faith: "But my daughter Hannah will take my place."

When her mother lay dying, moving in and out of pain, her iron-willed grandmother said to Hannah, "Promise your mother that you will stay at home and look after your father after she is no longer with us. You are the daughter called to this task. Promise her *now*."

Hannah later recalled, "My heart nearly stood still. I had been converted only one year, and had promised the Lord to go abroad as a missionary . . ." (HH).

In this most painful of situations—at her mother's deathbed—Hannah had to fight back the temptation to doubt. Was she really required to *stay at home*—ironically, the life she had once hoped to live—avoiding other people and giving in to her fears of the world?

"Promise, Hannah," her grandmother urged sternly. "You must set her mind at rest."

So Hannah put the question to her mother: "Mother, do you really want me to make this promise?"

When her mother opened her eyes wearily, the words came out in the Quaker speech that the Hurnards used with their children: "I thought thee felt the Lord was calling thee to be a missionary?"

"I do, I do," Hannah cried with a breaking heart. "You know I am training for it. I do believe he has called me."

"Then don't ever allow anything to hinder thee going," her mother said. "Do his will, whatever happens. Father wants that too" (HH).

Thus her mother, just as her father had done at Keswick, resolutely dedicated her daughter to the work to which Hannah herself now felt called.

Hannah was honest enough to admit that her fear of public speaking never totally left her. "Every time I got up to speak before others," she later wrote, "I felt it was impossible. And for years all the wretched physical sensations and accompaniments of fear remained. But strangely enough this was never apparent, and people often said to me, 'Don't you ever feel nervous when you are speaking in public? You seem to do it so easily'" (HH).

It was almost as though each challenge to speak for her Lord brought her once again to the place of sacrifice, to the altar of obedience. And each time, she would find herself choosing again to "go forward, acting as though I could actually see him beside me, see his understanding smile, and hear his reassuring voice saying, 'My grace is sufficient for thee, for my strength is made perfect in weakness.'"

So it was that Hannah's fears and speech impediment repeatedly brought her to her knees before God. She later recognized, "These very handicaps which had threatened to wreck my whole life were now my greatest safeguards and blessings. . . . The two handicaps which had so tormented me were, in reality, two special love gifts from the Lord." For it is in our weakness that we are reminded who speaks through us and for whose sake we live.

To see our infirmities as "love gifts" from God is a pinnacle of faith and commitment for which many of us strive. Yet Hannah, even in the early days of her dedication to a life of preaching the gospel, saw clearly how her weaknesses could be used in God's service. The glow in her eyes and her newly relaxed demeanor made her faith more evident to those around her as well. She was amazed and awed when one of her fellow students at Ridgelands said to her, "I almost envy you your stammer, Hannah, it seems to keep you so close to him, and make him so real to you."

She would later write, "Of course, really, we all start equally handicapped, though our handicaps differ in kind. Capable, self-confident people with wisdom and much common sense have to learn faith too, and to keep turning their own talents and abilities into utter dependence upon God. *Natural strength is often as great a handicap as natural weakness;* both must be utterly yielded to the Lord" (HH).

In the wake of this victory over stuttering, Hannah became further aware of her other faults: a temper, irritability, selfishness. Once, back at home, one of her sisters challenged her: "*How* have you changed? You're still the same old Hannah to me." It was a blow to Hannah that all of the signs of her newfound faith were not physically, obviously evident to those who knew her so closely. She swallowed hard and realized that in some ways she would always be a beginner, that with each triumph come new tasks and awarenesses that humble us further. This is God's way.

With resignation, but also a fresh anticipation, Hannah began to face the future. In 1926, at age twenty-one, she graduated from Ridgelands Bible College. Decisions had to be made about beginning some practical work for God's kingdom. Acknowledging that God had given her, along with painful problems, many natural strengths, Hannah took the next step of faith. Enthusiastically, she decided to join the Friends' Evangelistic Band and to strive to become, as their motto proclaimed, Ready for Anything.

Five

READY
FOR
ANYTHING

And a main road will go through that once-
deserted land; it will be named "The Holy
Highway." . . . God will walk there with
you. . . . All sorrow and all sighing will be
gone forever; only joy and gladness will be
there.

Isaiah 35:8-10, TLB

Let us go
Forth to the waiting field;
And where thy choicest fruit trees grow,
Thy pruning knife now wield
That at thy will and through thy skill
Their richest store may yield.

from Hinds' Feet on High Places

I was twenty-one when I joined them, and rather embar
rassed and shocked my relatives by traveling about the
country in a caravan, holding open air meetings and
missions in village after village," Hannah would later
write in *Hearing Heart* of her time with the Friends' Evangelistic Band (FEB).

Hannah was first attracted to the FEB, an interdenomina-
tional faith mission, through George A. Fox, a man who
shared the name of the great founder of the Society of
Friends. This George Fox once said, "The story of the Lord's
amazing grace and faithfulness in unfolding His love-plan for
a life is a romance which is the heritage of every believer."
He was destined to have a major influence on young Hannah. Undoubtedly, his strongly held philosophy kindled in

41

her active and receptive mind the growing sense of an unfolding "romance" with her Lord, which would be the compelling theme behind her life of service. Later, her literary gifts would find purpose in recording this journey in her fictional work *Hinds' Feet on High Places*.

As a member of the Friends' Prayer League, Fox had felt led of God to bring together a small collection of men and women dedicated to visiting remote places in Great Britain, two by two, in an evangelistic effort of house-to-house visitation. In these difficult spots, they would seek to revitalize the spiritual climate, especially in areas where chapels or gospel meeting halls had been closed down due to lack of interest in worship. Their own enthusiastic efforts at open-air services, along with personal house calls, were to start things going again, especially encouraging Sunday school training for the children of each village. Thus, the Friends' Evangelistic Band was founded. (Later it would be called "Fellowship for Evangelising Britain's Villages.")

During Hannah's Bible college days, she had seen individual Christian workers talking to people on a street corner or trying to preach the gospel and hand out leaflets in a seemingly resistant environment. Though she also had had some experience witnessing to such people, the scene among the poor and shabby, the disinterested, and the hostile had repulsed her.

The open-air meetings in her parents' circles, to which she was accustomed, were a far cry from such exhausting labor among people who appeared not to care. She was most familiar with well-known speakers commanding rapt audiences, supported by well-dressed musical accompanists with the highest standards.

It is important to remember how rigid the class distinc-
tions were in the society of her day. They affected speech and
dress protocol and companionship and, especially, vocation.

*Can God also work among the lowly and bedraggled, reaching
"common" people for his glory?* she wondered as she first
became aware of the FEB's work. It seemed contradictory,
even embarrassing, to this young woman who possessed such
an awareness of class and had propriety and dignity bred into
her thinking. Yet a nagging thought pressed into her mind.
*Could God even be calling me to perhaps the most difficult mission
field of all—those hostile to the gospel?*

George Fox with his resolute Band just happened to be
living in Colchester, Hannah's hometown! She had been
praying earnestly for openness to wherever the path to full-
time mission work might lead. Here was an ideal opportunity.
*Wouldn't this be a chance to gain experience in witnessing to
unchurched people, the skeptical, the disinterested, even the antagonistic?* And did not these people need the message of
peace as much as had her troubled self before her own
conversion?

A terrible shudder raced through her body. Not only did
this prospect fail to thrill her, it sickened her. How could
Hannah, born into wealth and privilege, join with working-
class youth and become one with them in purpose, sharing
the gritty tasks that lay ahead? Yet the more she prayed, the
more certain she became that she would throw in her lot
with this dedicated group. Here she was—the daughter of a
wealthy, well-known, and respected religious man, privileged
and sheltered all her life from the worlds of poverty and
disgrace—preparing to leave the walls of safety to face rejec-
tion and derision.

Finally, when it became clear to her in her quiet time that God was still leading her, her body relaxed, and her mind began adjusting to the reality of this call. All of her objections fell away as she found herself accepted and bound for service in their company. She was learning that in Christ, there are no such barriers as class or age, male or female, for all are called to be "fools for Christ's sake" (1 Cor. 4:10).

Joining the FEB provided Hannah with the opportunity to do her much-desired itinerant evangelistic work, starting in Essex but soon going to help evangelize Irish villages. While her native terrain was flat with numerous fields and meadows, she found Ireland to be rich with sturdy hills, sparkling lakes, and rolling, green countryside. And it received far more rain than she was accustomed to!

The people were different as well. In the Celtic tradition, Irish folk were warm, volatile, noisy, and gregarious, compared to their more staid and proper—and highly independent—English counterparts. Little did Hannah know that the challenge of adjusting to new people, a strange climate, and many physical hardships would be a preparation for even greater difficulties in her future work.

In the early days of Hannah's travels with the FEB, there were about twenty workers who traveled in two horse caravans and one motor van. At the end of four years, the group had grown to nearly a hundred workers and forty caravans. Hannah's friend and fellow worker Susette Poole later wrote these recollections of her time with the FEB:

> Hannah became part of a bicycle group that had only one bicycle! We were to go to an open-air evangelistic meeting in another village, so one rode the bicycle so

far, and then left it on the roadside. The next person of the group walked to the bicycle, then rode it past the first rider, and so on!

Hannah also took her turn riding the bicycle to collect a bucketful of hot water from a kindly farmer along the way. Once she returned with that precious bucket, another person went for a second bucket of hot water for our washing needs—then maybe another person went for one load of cold water. No water stayed long in our caravan!

Once Hannah and Susette were asked to conduct a meeting at Meath Place, a Quaker mission among the less well-off in Dublin. On the way, they stopped in a shop to have tea, and Hannah spilled hers on her frock. At the meeting, Susette was speaking on God washing people "whiter than snow" when both young women suddenly saw the funny side of their earlier experience and started to giggle! It took several embarrassing moments for them to collect themselves.

Mr. Hurnard often invited his daughter and her fellow workers to his home in Colchester on their free Saturdays, as he said, "to stretch their arms and have a hot bath." This was a great joy to the workers and a kind act on his part.

Another highlight for Hannah and the others was returning each year to the Keswick Convention.

"Hannah always gave a wonderful testimony of her conversion," Susette later recalled—and she would tell it often at FEB meetings they held together.

Those return trips to Keswick also began to plant more deeply in Hannah's mind the very idea of *living on the High*

Places. For the Keswick founders both believed in and experienced in their lives an ever-increasing work of grace. They fully expected that faith would continually grow in a believer's heart, enabling him or her to learn to live on spiritual heights in a corrupt world. Hannah was learning what this meant in her first mission assignments.

One year Hannah and Susette attended the Quaker Yearly Meeting in Dublin. Relating a lighthearted incident that occurred, Susette later remembered, "We stayed with the lovely family of Harriet Bewley. Her sister, Miss Hill from Lurgan, who was also there, took an interest even in our appearance. She decided we should be more fashionably attired, and she gave me a hat to wear!"

Hannah spent the years from 1926 to 1930 with the FEB. Answering such a call, though demanding and exhausting, brought her into daily service "in the atmosphere of heaven," as she put it. To the formerly lonely young woman, the fellowship of others with a similar calling to dedicated Christian service was joy unthinkable.

The motto of the Band at that time was Ready for Anything. The fact that Hannah could then approach such arduous and outgoing work showed the deepening of love for others that had begun in her heart. She faced real challenges in the world of human need and suffering that the Band encountered. "Ready for Anything" meant that disciples were to have *hearing hearts* and *open eyes* to whatever the Lord called them to attempt in his name, no matter what people thought.

Susette's recollection of Hannah waking one morning to find a large pig rubbing itself against their caravan (a rich girl's temporary home!) was a refreshing reminder that spiritual work has its humble side. Surely we all need to live in the real world of discomforts and physical demands, even of humor, to keep us from taking ourselves too seriously.

"Notice among yourselves, dear brothers, that few of you who follow Christ have big names or power or wealth. Instead, God has deliberately chosen to use ideas the world considers foolish and of little worth in order to shame those people considered by the world as wise and great . . . so that no one anywhere can ever brag in the presence of God" (1 Cor. 1:26-27, 29, TLB).

Hannah expresses this paradox beautifully in her "Water Song," an original poem in *Hinds' Feet on High Places,* in which the Shepherd is seeking to explain to Much-Afraid how it is that we are called not only to High Places, but to the humblest places of all. We, too, must descend, as the water of a stream falls down to the lowest level—only at some point to rise into the most majestic of waterfalls:

> Come, oh come! let us away—
> Lower, lower every day,
> Oh, what joy it is to race
> Down to find the lowest place.
> This is the dearest law we know—
> "It is happy to go low."
> Sweetest urge and sweetest will,
> "Let us go down lower still."
>
> Hear the summons night and day
> Calling us to come away.
> From the heights we leap and flow
> To the valleys down below.
> Always answering to the call,

To the lowest place of all.
Sweetest urge and sweetest pain,
To go low and rise again.

"The High Places," the Shepherd explains, "are the starting places for the journey down to the lowest place in the
world. When you have hinds' feet and can go 'leaping on the
mountains and skipping on the hills,' you will be able, as I
am, to run down from the heights in gladdest self-giving and
then go up to the mountain again. . . . For it is only up on the
High Places of Love that anyone can receive the power to
pour themselves down in an utter abandonment of self-giving" (HF).

Exhausting daily work with the Band brought Hannah
mercifully outside of herself. She began to move more freely
in the open air and increasingly to sense her connection with
all creation. In this experience, she began to perceive the
paradox of the gospel itself: It is in lowly service that we
participate in the high call of God in Christ. And in this,
Christ himself is our example, for he "took upon him the
form of a servant, and . . . humbled himself, and became
obedient unto death, even the death of the cross." Therefore,
God has "highly exalted him, and given him a name which
is above every name: That at the name of Jesus every knee
should bow . . ." (Phil. 2:7-10).

The apostle Paul wrote to followers of the Way, during the
early life of the church and his own work as a missionary, "We
are fools for Christ's sake, . . . we are weak . . . [and] despised"
(1 Cor. 4:10). "It was lovely to be a fool for Christ's sake,"
Hannah would later write of those years, "and we were filled
with a radiant joy whenever others were persuaded to follow

him too. I know the wonder of it used to break over me in waves of thankfulness. . . . I could hardly believe that I was the same miserable, morbid person who had longed to commit suicide and escape from the world altogether. And it was the Lord Jesus who had made all the difference" (HH).

Evangelizing in areas where Christian fervor had died out, where churches and chapels were practically empty, had its particular obstacles. The workers asked themselves, What would best demonstrate to indifferent or antagonistic people that Christ lived and was reaching out to them through these enthusiastic but inexperienced young people? Open-air meetings held in a village street were real attention-getters, as difficult as they often were to manage, with only two workers in a locale.

At these street meetings, Hannah would play the portable harmonium while her partner sang hymns; the two would take turns preaching at what seemed a street nearly devoid of people! But a careful observer would see windows down the street cautiously opening to allow eyes to gaze out at the odd sight and to enable ears to listen. Then some ragged children might start to appear. And Hannah and her partner would stoop down to teach them Christian choruses and invite them to children's meetings in a nearby chapel—the use of which they had already secured from a local vicar who, typically, was happy to oblige out of gratitude for the young people's assistance.

Often Hannah was simply tired. The progress of the Band seemed slow and discouraging. Then, when priceless opportunities to meet with individuals cropped up either through the open-air preaching or the door-to-door visitation, amazingly, she would be revived. Once, she reports, when she and her partner were in a village that seemed to have a spiritual void, she was out witnessing alone. She approached a "miserable cottage where, I had been told, a fallen woman was living with the third or fourth man for whom she had kept house." When the young woman answered the door, Hannah was shocked to see a thin, sad, and unkempt young girl about her own age. But her heart was moved with pity.

"Please excuse me, but I have come to tell you about the Lord Jesus and the wonderful way he can help you," Hannah began. Somehow overlooking the dirt and squalor, and suppressing her own squeamishness at the sight of the poor cottage and its weed-infested garden, she managed to communicate the gospel.

"You are a good girl, aren't you?" the young woman asked her. "You don't know what it is to be bad. Oh, I wish I were good too." At that she burst into tears, turned her back to Hannah, and escaped into her cottage. Although Hannah never knew what effect she might have had on the girl's situation, the encounter profoundly affected her own heart. "Why am I not in her place and she in mine? Why has God's grace so delivered and transformed me, and she and so many multitudes of others don't know anything about it?" (HH).

From this and other experiences, Hannah learned how dependent she must be, on a day-to-day basis, upon sitting in the presence of God. This lifeline was necessary for her to see any results at all. She began to appreciate anew the Quaker emphasis on the phrase *hearing heart*—which she would later use as the title of her autobiography. Also, she saw the need for close and happy fellowship with her coworkers and the importance of confessing faults, one to another, in preparation for prayerful guidance.

Like all the Band workers, Hannah frequently changed witnessing partners. Always, they were living in cramped caravan quarters with new adjustments to make. This and other hardships kept them constantly seeking God's help in all the details of their life, both spiritual and physical. Upon returning to their caravan following a difficult day of personal visitation, she and her partner consciously practiced these agreed-upon principles. They sought as much harmony as possible in desire and method, so that their prayer times together were like gentle conversations with God while sitting as children in his presence.

When you pray regularly with other people, "however different you may be temperamentally or in outlook and background, you cannot help loving the people you pray with," Hannah later wrote (HIH), and you learn to adapt yourself to their way of life. She knew the feel and taste of Jesus' words that "where two or three are gathered together in my name, there am I in the midst of them" (Matt. 18:20).

Her miraculous conversion had prepared Hannah well to have ears to hear and eyes to see. From sitting at the feet of her Savior in quiet contemplation and meditation, she possessed an almost untiring yearning to know more about spiritual realities and truths. By her own admission, she remained extremely uninterested in the practical, humdrum drudgery of daily life.

Hannah's cooking disasters, for example, were notorious. She failed even at preparing the simple fare that the partners were to share at meals, typically letting the others do it all. But some of them refused to let her off that easily, so she was forced to learn basic culinary skills. She only changed so much, though. A certain partner's continual complaints of stomachaches from Hannah's dishes, meant that Hannah had a break from cooking for a while! Eventually, she found herself appropriately paired with another young woman who also was, Hannah later remembered, "a hopeless cook and just as uninterested in household things as I was." They were quite happy together and, fortunately, found themselves asked out frequently to meals at the homes of villagers. To their surprise, those occasions at guest tables offered opportunities for a greater witness—and even their shortcomings became the tools of ministry!

Hannah was a true Mary, rather than a Martha. She preferred having someone there to make any necessary arrangements and do perfunctory chores, thus treating (actually, pampering) her as she was accustomed to in her precollege years. For instance, sometimes Hannah relied on her witnessing partners' greater experience in the world by asking them to do things for her because she felt they were "beyond her." "I was two days older than Hannah," Susette later recalled with a smile, "so she would suggest that I buy our train tickets and attend to such details, due to my great age!" In this regard, God had a further work to do in Hannah that she would have happily avoided.

Later, Hannah was to find more balance in her life between spiritual and physical needs. She would write of this, "It was a long time before my heart learned to hear my Lord's voice telling me his will about such mundane things as washing up [dish washing], dusting, and trying to be tidy. But how patiently he bore with me, and with what faithful friends and fellow workers he has always put me."

She learned, too, that physical and spiritual needs sometimes overlap and cannot be so easily separated—and that

Ready for Anything takes both kinds into account. Hannah was once sent to a little village named Angel Bank located in Shropshire. There she became part of an effort to hold a mission in an almost-deserted chapel belonging to the Ludlow Methodist Circuit. One local pastor and his wife offered hospitality and their home to the mission team. It was a "tiny two-roomed cottage, which stood all alone, far from the main road, and in order to reach it we had to climb three sets of steps." The one bedroom, which the couple generously gave up to the workers' use, was reached by a stepladder through a trapdoor in the ceiling of the kitchen! A single cow supplied the couple's milk and dairy products. Unfortunately, this animal became ill and needed treatments throughout the cold autumn. When a cold spell set in, it was made worse by a long, drawn-out coal strike, which was reflected in the cottage's dwindling store of fuel in the yard. Hannah and her partner saw their hosts grow more and more anxious as conditions worsened.

One day Hannah descended from the little upstairs room to find their hostess in tears. "Oh, Miss Hurnard," she said. "I don't know what we are to do. The last little piece of coal and coal dust are on the fire now, and we can get no more wood. I have boiled a kettle to make a pot of tea for our breakfast, but there is nothing left with which to cook our dinner, and the cow will not be able to have her treatment and will surely die.

"My husband was in Ludlow several days ago trying to order coal, but because of this strike there is none to be had, and there won't be any for nobody knows how long."

Hannah stiffened. She was appalled to come face-to-face with such wrenching need. They ate their meager breakfast.

Then, with no tangible hope of a later meal, she and her partner climbed back up to their room to pray. Hannah's heart was sinking, but her partner, the senior worker of the Band, was expectant and positive, and prayed, "O Heavenly Father, thou knowest the real need there is for more coal. Don't let these kindly friends suffer as a result of their hospitality to us, through using up their little store of coal on our account. And please, don't let their cow die."

To make up for her own lack of faith in this desperate situation, Hannah could only manage a sincere "Amen" in affirmation. Her inexperience with neediness made her particularly vulnerable to doubt. Though she had read about such miracles in tracts, she could hardly believe they happened in real life!

The coldness of the house was a tangible, relentless presence. It continued to seep into their living quarters. Wrapped in too-thin blankets, she and her partner felt increasingly uncomfortable—their muscles tightening and their teeth chattering—as they prayed.

Later in the day, when only a small flame still flickered in the kitchen grate, an answer came. Their excited hostess suddenly exclaimed, "Oh, look, there's a coal cart arriving just now!" All of the women hurried outside. The good news was confirmed. Supplies had been sent—from heaven—by way of a local delivery. A few truckloads of coal, the man with the cart explained, *had* reached Ludlow the day before, and this was their bounty.

The pastor happily built up the cottage fire. The cow got its treatments and recovered. And a long-awaited hot meal was lovingly prepared for all by the hostess. In celebration, everyone gratefully sat down to a welcome table. The Lord's faithful workers and their hosts experienced the provision they had prayed for, in the hour of their greatest need. And the work of the kingdom in that place could go on.

Another time, when traveling in West Ireland, Hannah and a partner prepared to hold meetings in an empty chicken coop—which they cleaned out, disinfected, and decorated with flowers. It was a risk because a male team working in the region earlier had been attacked—one member had been fired at while in their van. The vehicle still had bullet holes when Hannah and her partner took it over. But it was felt that women evangelists would not be subject to that kind of aggression, and fortunately this proved to be true. The mission was to be successful, yet there were other difficulties.

Material needs again hampered spiritual goals. One weekend the women workers had nothing to eat for an evening meal but bread and tea. While they prayed simply for "something else," a knock came at the door. When they opened it, they received a package from Dublin—far across the country—containing a plump roast fowl wrapped in still-crisp cabbage leaves.

Thus, Ready for Anything came to mean even more to Hannah: a full stomach, as well as a thankful heart; deliverance from cold and discomfort; provision for the day; hope for further service tomorrow; and, above all, a heavenly Father who knows the needs of his children even before the request leaves their lips. Hannah was learning important lessons in her own Valley of Loss and Deprivation—how material blessings are never to be taken for granted, but always received as gifts of God's bounty. And prayers for physical sustenance, she learned, should always include petitions for the necessary pruning and growth of one's character.

Sometimes both would come at the same time. Thus, the pattern for her spiritual walk was confirmed. From then on, she would ask God to provide, wait on him for answers, and, in everything, give thanks.

Six

"WILL YOU GO TO MY PEOPLE?"

And it shall come to pass in the last days, that the mountain of the Lord's house shall be established in the top of the mountains, and shall be exalted above the hills; and all nations shall flow unto it. And many people shall go and say, Come ye, and let us go up to the mountain of the Lord, to the house of the God of Jacob; and he will teach us of his ways, and we will walk in his paths: for out of Zion shall go forth the law, and the word of the Lord from Jerusalem.

Isaiah 2:2-3

"Are you willing to leave your bones in Palestine, if necessary, Miss Hurnard?"

from Hearing Heart

I f you cut a tulip bulb in sections for the microscope you can find the whole complete plant and flower that is to be. Hidden within that bulb are to be found the leaves, the petals, the stamens, the pistil, and even the miniature grains of pollen.

"How can the beauty of form and colour be brought to perfection according to the Divine plan? There is only one way. The bulb must be placed where the Divine purpose can operate unhindered."*

*Quoted by Bessie Bryers in *To Them That Obey* (Colchester, England: Fellowship for Evangelising Britain's Villages, 1969, p. 45).

These wise words were written by George Fox, founder of the Friends' Evangelistic Band, in which Hannah got her start as an evangelistic worker. And they could hardly apply more accurately than in Hannah's own story.

During her last year with the Band, Hannah, then twenty-four, began earnestly to seek out where she was to be "planted" in her chosen vocation as a minister of the gospel.

Despite many glorious experiences with the FEB, Hannah never found the Band's methods comfortable or its challenges easy. She chafed at eating and sleeping in a caravan's cramped quarters as well as having little or no privacy. Some mornings she would wake up simply feeling too *weak* to get her young body to move. She was also plagued by chronic anemia, feverish chills, and prostrating neuralgic headaches.

Why not simply leave and go pursue a less demanding form of service? she sometimes thought. Though she loved the Band and its work, part of her would have preferred a life of fewer discomforts, more successes, and less monotonous hardship. There she was, traveling down long, dark, muddy country roads, carrying few supplies, and trusting by faith that the next village would offer some welcome. It all began to wear on her more and more.

Yet as she was to look back on the four years spent in the Ready for Anything company of other enthusiastic young people and leaders, she would admit that the experience had been the best possible preparation for the particular work to which God would later call her.

In 1930, while she was completing her fourth year with the Band, Hannah was sent to Ireland once again to do deputation work—telling of the needs of the unevangelized villages of England and Ireland and raising financial and prayer support for the ministries there. One Saturday afternoon during this trip, she found herself invited to go along with a party of young factory- and shop-working women to a small and beautiful island northeast of Dublin, known as Ireland's Eye.

Carrying with her a light jacket, her Bible, and her notebook, she set out to be alone for a time. She sat silently, basking in the beauty of nature, where she always felt most at home. Against a deep blue sky, the starkly white seagulls soared above the rocky coast while she gazed, transfixed. As the successive rhythm of the Irish Sea surf rose up and washed over the shoreline, serenity came over her. There Hannah felt again, as she had on so many occasions, true communion with her Creator—the Maker of all things and lover of her soul. Her heart was lifted. A lonely figure on a rocky slope, she once more opened herself to discerning God's will.

She remembered Abraham—that wherever he traveled and God met him, he built an altar. Hannah too longed to build another altar, to offer herself wholly again to the Lord, ready for whatever he might be wanting her to do. When she turned to her Bible, she had no special subject in mind, so she began to read just where the Bible opened, which happened to be Daniel 9. At once she saw that it described how Daniel—the "man greatly beloved" by his God—went apart to pray to the Lord. At once she was struck by the amazing way in which he *completely identified himself with his nation in their sin and their rebellion against God*, for which they had been carried into captivity. But Daniel himself had not sinned. From the first, he had refused to worship idols, even after having been carried away captive to one of the most wicked and idolatrous courts in the world. Yet here he was, praying as one completely identified with God's people in their sin and need of God's pardon and restoration.

Thoroughly engrossed, Hannah slowly read to herself Daniel's prayer: "O Lord, hear; O Lord, forgive; . . . defer not, for thine own sake, O my God: for thy city and thy people are called by thy name" (v. 19). She marveled at the passion of humility and longing love that made this wonderful and holy man able to identify himself so completely with his rebellious and backsliding people, the Jews.

Then, like a bolt from the flawless sky, an astonishing awareness of God's presence came to Hannah. As the dazzlingly bright sunlight struck her eyes and seemed to touch her very heart, a thought came into her mind with perfect clarity and a significance that seemed directly drawn from the reading that had so affected her: *Hannah, would you be willing to identify yourself with the Jewish people in the same way, if I asked you to?*

She was stunned. *Hannah, will you go to my people?* was the direct and earth-shattering question her Lord was unmistakably asking.

Hannah knew a few things about the history of the area God seemed to be leading her to. Less than one hundred years earlier, while the Holy Land was under Turkish control, the Moslem Turkish sultan had to be appealed to whenever a Jewish subject wished to change religion. In 1846, the sultan made a ruling that was to enable the British and other European missionaries to make converts legally: He allowed a young Jewish boy to confess his faith in Jesus and to be baptized at the British Mission, which was then called the London Jews Society (LJS).

The very first Christians in the early church had, of course, been Jewish. All of the Gospel writers, except Luke, were of the Lord's own *chosen* people. Yet, through the years, the Jews had been dispersed from their native land of Israel and had suffered at the hands of oppressors throughout the world. During the Crusades—from the early eleventh century well into the thirteenth—Jews had even been unjustly executed by misguided segments of the Christian church.

Through decades of struggle, the British missionary community had firmly established an ongoing work in the Holy Land. Believers were literally worshiping and proclaiming God's Word on the mountain of the Lord, at Mount Zion. German Protestant missionaries also cooperated with the British workers, especially in providing medical treatment to the needy. The message of eternal life for all who would believe was able to go forth and bear fruit as hearts were opened to Christ through the kindness and concern of those who served.

Unfortunately, there was always strife among the peoples of Palestine, which made life difficult for anyone called to minister there. Only the year before, 1929, her father had taken Hannah and her older brother for a two-month tour of the Holy Land, beginning at Aleppo in the north of Syria and ending with a stay in Palestine. An extremely wealthy man, Samuel Hurnard was free to travel and support Christian missionary work. Samuel had for some time been deeply interested in the Armenian refugee camps that existed at that time in Syria. He had also wanted to see some of the new Jewish settlements in Palestine, which he believed to be a

63

marvelous fulfillment of biblical prophecy. For him, this represented an astonishing step toward that final day when Jesus shall reign in "the city of the Great King," as ruler over the whole earth (see 1 Thess. 4:16; Zech. 12:10; 14:9).

Hannah and her brother had been delighted to visit and observe so many of the places of which they had read in the Bible, especially to walk the hills of Galilee and alongside the lake there. But the young people had less interest in visiting modern Jewish agricultural sites and chose to go off on their own to the open country or the sparkling shore whenever their father planned to observe the settlements. Both found the modern manifestation of Zionism unattractive, and Hannah had found herself filled with an inner antipathy toward those Jewish people she met. *I don't care for them, and I'm glad I don't have to live among them,* she had thought at the time.

Now, as she sat on Ireland's Eye contemplating Palestine as a mission field, she thought of the new town of Tel Aviv, built on the sand in that historic country, and the realities of day-to-day service in such a place.

These words came to her again: *Hannah, are you willing to go to Palestine and live and work among the Jews, and identify yourself with them completely?*

Her answer surprised her in its strength and negativity. "But, Lord, I'm sorry to say I don't like the Jews a bit. They are the last people in the world I feel interested in trying to help. How could I be of any use as a missionary to the Jews if I don't like them?"

The answer came: *If you will yield to me wholly and agree to go, I will make you able to love them and identify yourself with them. It all depends upon your will* (HH).

In a later work of hers entitled *Thou Shalt Remember*, Hannah would write of this dialogue with God:

> "Lord! . . . Why do you ask me to go there? . . . Lord Jesus, why Palestine? Why Jews? Why Arabs?"
>
> "Because I was a Jew myself," said the Lord Jesus, "and I suffered there for you and for all the world. Will you go back there, Hannah, and let me teach you how to love . . . so that you may become more and more like me?"

She looked down at the mossy rock before which she had knelt, unaware, and realized that there on that glorious sunny day on Ireland's Eye, it had become an altar. Her only words were: "Here I am, Lord. I will go as a missionary to your people, Israel."

Though at that time she more strongly identified herself with the righteous Daniel, she was, through the years, increasingly to begin to identify herself with the people to whom she was sent. But her understanding on her commissioning day was enough to bring the smile of a *yes* to her lips, while her heart "glowed with an awed and amazed joy," as she would later describe it.

Later, after having come down from the "mountaintop," she found it difficult to communicate the assurance she felt within to her friends and fellow workers. When she began to tell her colleagues of the direction she had received from God while up on the rocky peak, they were dubious. There was so little concrete evidence to show that this was indeed God's will for Hannah's life. She could only vaguely refer them to Daniel 9 and her excitement about the challenge of Palestine.

ıy with us, Hannah. This is where you have been sent, and the work is prospering." The leader of the Band at first tried to keep her with its company longer. Surely God was using her and blessing her work in that very country! And perhaps, others suggested, she was not strong enough to serve in such a hot, merciless climate as Palestine.

As Hannah was contemplating this move, she continued to learn lessons about grace and glory. She was being called to have faith in the concept that the road to God's best often involves risks and difficulties one would surely never choose. For Hannah, being sent to a hostile mission field meant a further shedding of her natural pride and sense of "correctness." She later wrote, "I think very few true disciples of the Lord Jesus are allowed always to appear sensible and correct. We all have to appear as fools in the eyes of the world at some time or other. For, after all, pride is the greatest cause of unbelief and . . . looking foolish is one of the ways by which we take up the cross and crucify our pride" (HH).

Hannah's first inquiry about work in Palestine was to the secretary of the Church Missions to Jews (CMJ, today known as Church's Ministry Among the Jews), which she knew did wonderful work in the Holy Land.

The mission had originally been established as the London Society for Promoting Christianity among the Jews. It was first a Free Church society; later it was associated with the Anglican Church. It held as its aim "to send our missionaries in and out amongst the Jews, bringing the remnant according to grace into the fellowship of the gospel, and preparing the nation as a whole for that great day when the Jews shall . . . acknowledge Him as their Messiah."

Hannah felt sure that this was the band of faithful workers that God was calling her to join next. With enthusiasm she filled out the CMJ form, sent it in, and waited hopefully for a response. A disappointing letter came back. "Since at present you have no special qualifications as a nurse, a teacher, or a secretary"—all of which *were* needed in that particular field—there were no apparent ministry opportunities. There was, sadly but perhaps not surprisingly, "no opening for a lady evangelist." Among the Jews, she was told, women were not generally considered worth listening to if they tried to preach to or teach men. Hannah at that time seemed not to realize how unusual it was for a young woman of her background and age (twenty-five at the time), untrained in a specific professional skill, to even want to apply for such work.

However, there was one note of hope in the letter. In a few months' time, Dr. James Churcher, who worked for a sister society to CMJ and was a venerable figure in British Evangelicalism, would be traveling to England on furlough. At that time, if she still felt led to that country's needs, she was invited to apply again. When Dr. Churcher arrived, Hannah went to see the wise and dedicated man. He smiled down at her, beaming goodwill. But he was honest and cautioned her carefully about any illusions she might have about working in the Holy Land.

"You must consider the climate of Haifa," Dr. Churcher told her kindly. Continually hot and damp, it took its toll on workers. Nervous breakdowns were common, and he warned, "It is not a place for the faint-hearted." He emphasized, too, that they did not want temporary or short-term people, but rather those who would look on the work as their life's calling, to be endured through inevitable hardship.

"Are you willing to leave your bones in Palestine, if necessary, Miss Hurnard?" he asked her softly yet pointedly. This was a challenge to total, lifelong dedication: to following Christ, whatever it might require of her, to the death if it should be. Was she ready?

Hannah swallowed hard. To one who had just come from such an altar of commitment, and as a young woman trusting her Lord, there could only be one answer. She slowly and carefully replied that if the Lord's second coming did not intervene, "Yes, I would be willing to die there if necessary."

Yet Dr. Churcher persisted: "What makes you suppose that God is calling you to work among Jews in Palestine? Why not Jews in London, or in Europe, or perhaps in Egypt? Have you thought, for instance, of offering to help in the school for Jews in Cairo?"

Hannah responded softly that she had not, as she had not been trained as a teacher, and to her, the call had been clear: Go to Palestine.

Determined to make her face reality, Dr. Churcher continued. "Look here, we do need a trained nurse and a secretary—but not, at this time, an untrained gap-filler. We don't want you to make a serious mistake. Please go back and bring your desire to the Lord once again, as though you had not already received a call. If it becomes confirmed to you through prayer, we will talk again. Forget the glamour of the Holy Land, as people think about it in their minds. Perhaps instead you will receive a call to London or Cairo."

So Hannah returned to her home, feeling inadequate to follow through on what she felt was truly her call to Palestine and the Jews there—so clearly received on Ireland's Eye. She crept to her room and there prayed fervently. "Oh, please, Lord Jesus, do teach and guide me. Make me sure of thy will! Is it really Palestine, or some other place where I may reach Jews for you?"

Close to tears, she opened her Bible again, and at once her eyes fell upon God's call to Moses: "Come now therefore, and I will send thee unto . . . Egypt" (Exod. 3:10). She could not help laughing!

"Lord," she prayed, "if you meant me to go to the school for Jewish children in Cairo, why wasn't I led into training earlier as a teacher, to prepare me?" Yet soon an assurance came over her that she had *not* missed her chance for the right training. Just opening the Bible and letting it fall open to a verse—though God had worked through this method to guide her before—was not enough. There had to be other clear signs of specific leading as to God's *total plan* for one's work and life, she realized. This is a wise and important understanding.

Hannah's own father at this point became a compass and a guide to the sincere and searching young woman. He was truly delighted and affirming when Hannah told him she believed that God was calling her to work among Jews in Palestine.

"Thy mother and I," he said in Quaker phrasing, "dedicated thee to the Lord before thou wast born, and we always hoped that the Lord would call thee, if it were his will, to work among the Jews" (HH). Many years later he was to write her in a precious letter that her decision to go to Palestine as an evangelist against all the odds was one of the greatest blessings of his life.

69

This confirmation—being reminded of her parents' dedi-cation of her to this specific work—now reinforced Hannah's own desire and dedication, so recently realized.

Hannah also remembered her mother's final words to her. She acknowledged God's beautiful timing in giving her such kinship with her mother and her mother's work, which was to be carried on in a new way, in a new land, but with the joy of true fulfillment. How glad Hannah was that a mother who had borne with an unhappy, even morbid, daughter, through years of discontent, could have afterward welcomed her to a life of dedicated Christian service!

The time had come for Hannah to act. The reasons from her past were enough evidence to convince her that she should and would go.

New challenges, however, stymied her. *What can I do that is any different from the other, more skilled laborers?* she won-dered. As she had no specific skills to offer, she agreed to go to Haifa at her own expense and to undertake to prove her worth. She would fill in gaps wherever she might be required until it would be revealed how the Lord planned to use *her*. She could not expect a wary mission to take her on as a salaried employee when they had no opening for one with her evangelistic experience and skills—and who was *a woman*, at that.

Hannah was back at square one, a humbling place for one so straight-backed and strong, so full of fervor and stubborn determination. "Oh, how deeply thankful I was to the mis-sion, and how thankful I have remained ever since," she would write in *Hearing Heart*, "for the loving, patient way they accepted me during those first difficult years abroad when I could do so little for them.

70

"In the end," she wrote of her surrender at age twenty-six, "I crept meekly, and oh, so thankfully, into Palestine on January 21, 1932. And what a stripping and breaking process then began."

Seven

IN THE
LAND OF
PROMISE

*And thine ears shall hear a word behind thee,
saying, This is the way, walk ye in it, when ye
turn to the right hand, and when ye turn to the
left.*

Isaiah 30:21

*The Shepherd explained to Much-Afraid
gently: "That is the path, Much-Afraid, and
you are to go down there."*

*"Oh, no," she cried. "You can't mean it. You
said if I would trust you, you would bring me
to the High Places, and that path leads right
away from them. It contradicts all that you
promised."*

*"No," said the Shepherd, "it is not contra-
diction, only postponement for the best to become possible."*

from Hinds' Feet on High Places

H er tired body responded to the piercing alarm clock as
though it would split her very being in two. *How could
it be morning already?* Hannah thought resentfully. Squinting
at the half-light from the window, she rolled slowly out of
bed, lifted her arms, and stretched. Then she sighed.

She desired to put God first, to seek only his will again for
yet another day. However, now that she was at the Haifa clinic
to work "on trial" as an unpaid medical assistant, the realities
of this chosen life were coming home to her. Today her whole
body seemed unwilling to conform to her inner wishes.

Finally she was in the "Land of Promise"—Palestine. The rising sun's bright light startled her. Revealed before her eyes was a landscape of many contrasts, ancient and new, living side by side. The geographical splendors of the terrain over which Jesus had walked and ministered were daily sights for Hannah. Four enduring seas marked the boundaries of this country: the Mediterranean, immediately to the west; the Red Sea, to the south; and the Dead Sea and the Sea of Galilee, along the east. From the soaring seagull to the coiling snake, life teemed in a variety of forms.

In spite of the region's beauty and vitality, Hannah sometimes felt misplaced. Tired, and even depressed, she was discovering that life here was far more demanding than she had ever imagined.

It is one thing joyfully to agree to go forth to the mission field, in answer to a specific call, *ready for anything*. It is quite another to encounter the gritty and particular difficulties of missionary life.

"I don't know whether I will be able to withstand this climate!" she often sighed to herself. Her weariness was reflected in her eyes as she glanced into a small mirror. Having made few friends, she already had serious doubts about the future.

Nevertheless, Hannah's clear sense of purpose and deep commitment to her quiet time with her Shepherd sustained her through the difficult first four years in Haifa. A new life of servanthood in "gap-filling" had opened up for her. It would expose her shortcomings as well as more sharply define her distinct calling received on Ireland's Eye. What would follow this "apprenticeship" would be revealed by God only *after* more lessons were learned.

The top floor of the large mission house contained the apartment she shared with two foreign deaconesses or nursing "sisters." One woman was from Finland and the other from Germany. Together, the three traveled daily to the large clinic a little over a mile away in a horse-drawn, two-wheeled carriage. The doctor rode in on horseback.

In Israel the rainy seasons are noted for their tremendous downpours. As an additional hardship, the winter of 1931–32 brought unusually heavy snows. During May and October the "hamseens," or desert winds, blow from the dry regions, causing inhabitants to have difficulties maintaining stamina and normal breathing. In summer the shoreline at Haifa was extremely humid.

Hannah found the brutal contrasts of the hot, damp climate debilitating. It usually left her listless and exhausted. Minor discomforts kept her continually irritated, weary, and aching. Never did she feel quite well. Seldom was she able to sleep soundly. She frequently would begin to toss on her thin, uncomfortable mattress as the morning approached, realizing that she would need to rise early—sometimes at four o'clock—in order to prepare to offer any kind of service for her Lord.

Struggling with herself at that difficult hour, she found simply rising in good spirits to be a test of her endurance. Yet, once faced, the morning was often a beautiful gift. In late spring, dew droplets beaded the branches of olive trees. At times the sky seemed almost golden, as though God was speaking to her right through the screen of heaven and giving her a taste of the beauty of the first day of creation. Songbirds called out, and all the world seemed new. Hannah would smile and begin to feel refreshed. She intended to maintain the practice of the morning "tryst" with God that she had begun on the day of her conversion. This centering of her mind on God's will and the infusing of her soul with his strength was of prime importance. Without it, she knew she would be *powerless* to exemplify the kind of transforming relationship with Jesus that she had been introduced to and wished to help others discover.

While God had so miraculously made it possible for her to become a "filler-in," a worker of multiple functions, her true vocation was yet to be revealed. Hannah was eager for the opportunity to exercise her skill in witnessing and speaking in this land too. She was realizing, however, that even with her favored upbringing, her innate intelligence, and her single-mindedness for the gospel ministry, she was increasingly being asked to take a lower place.

Why cannot I begin the work of door-to-door evangelism to which I really *feel called?* she pleaded daily with her Lord.

One real barrier that Hannah recognized was her lack of language skills. Her older apartment mates talked mostly in their own languages, which left her feeling out in the cold. Nevertheless, they were kind as well as tolerant of her inexperience. Hannah's duties at the clinic were limited too. She had to face the truth: She was totally inadequate to attempt gospel teaching or ministry with her language handicap.

Medically untrained, she worked unceasingly on such mundane tasks as cleaning and sterilizing equipment. The operating and maintenance conditions were far from ideal, and she usually was needed to assist other, more qualified workers. Hannah frequently asked herself where was God's promise that *she would be used* in a strategic ministry in this place. She struggled to adapt her thinking and let God work through even the simplest tasks she was called upon to perform. For the sake of persevering, she stifled her inner, complaining heart as best she could.

Numerous small tragedies walked through the clinic's corridors daily. Often children had not received attention early enough to prevent serious illness; the men's and women's faces conveyed poverty and need—even hopelessness. Hannah earnestly cared for each patient's pains and difficulties. Even more, she wanted to reach them emotionally and spiritually, in their world of grief and need, so alien to her own privileged background. She wondered how.

Hannah continued to be strong-willed, independent, and commanding, despite the rigors of the climate. An overpowering desire for order and precision in the work, at all costs, consumed her. She found that these compulsions for exactness and reasonableness continually warred against her goal of expressing *compassion*. She knew that *loving* her patients was the best way to express God's love for these people—if only God would work *through her*.

A waiting room full of needy people—some ragged, shy children clinging to their mothers' skirts, bearded men looking frail and undernourished, yet proud and determined—the whole range of humanity, for whom Christ had died, was the scene of her daily work. She longed to be God's servant in their midst. One of her duties was sitting there and giving English lessons to any who wished to learn. As a text, Hannah read from the English translation of the Holy Bible; but it was difficult to teach modern English usage from that version's archaic phrasings. Anyway, most of the reasons people sought help in language centered around getting better jobs. So Hannah sought to bring the biblical truths to these "students" in the context of their typical daily experiences. Creatively, she devised lessons in which she jumped from selected passages in the four biographies of Jesus to everyday sentences that would help students communicate with English bosses. "For the kingdom of heaven is like a landowner . . ." (Matt. 20:1, NKJV) is one example. She employed New Testament parables such as the ones about vineyards and sheep.

This approach seemed to satisfy and even maintain the interest of her "classes," for they were in the very land of Jesus. The conditions of climate and custom under which he had spoken his words were understood. Furthermore, they were learning the Scriptures. And Hannah learned some Hebrew from her students in the process of providing a service and aiding the mission. In this the clinic staff greatly encouraged her.

One day Hannah was helping direct a few groups of incoming patients, while inviting others to her Bible class. Suddenly, a surly, unkempt man stalked demandingly into the waiting room. Though he didn't look sick, he announced that he was suffering from a skin irritation, which caused his whole body to itch miserably. While the other patients stared, the man rudely shouted out his need and demanded to see the doctor immediately. He looked to Hannah as though he might simply explode at any moment.

Hannah did her best to calm the stranger in order to protect the rights of the other patients who were scheduled for treatment before him. However, at one point, although she was not that strong, she had to bar the door to keep him back. The indignity of being a sort of "bouncer" hit her forcefully. She chafed spiritually at finding herself caught between many angry people and feeling overwhelmingly sure that she was the wrong person in the wrong place. *Have I somehow misunderstood God's call? It is practically impossible,* she despaired inwardly, *for me to experience the graciousness and love of a true servant of God in this place!*

Clenching her teeth, she attempted to restrain the man another minute. Just when she felt she could hold on no longer, the door behind her opened and the doctor said he would take the man at once. Relieved of the intense situation, Hannah could no longer hold back her own emotions. Though she spoke not a word out loud, her anger flared up toward the doctor. *How dare he take this ungrateful man ahead of the also-needy, regularly scheduled patients!* She had put forth all her strength to maintain order for nothing, she thought.

Later, in shame, she asked God to quiet her spirit, give her patience, and relieve her of her need to *control* and keep a schedule at the cost of compassion. In this case her will was to be surrendered for the sake of a desperately needy man who was in debilitating pain. Amazingly, after having received his treatment, the man came back to speak to Hannah.

"I am so embarrassed at my behavior . . . please forgive me!" he explained falteringly, with broken words. "I just go crazy when I'm itching all over. Until I can get the ointment, I'm another person. Now I can see what I was doing—I had no right . . ."

The proud assistant-in-charge felt her heart melt at the humanness of another soul. Remarkably, the two became friends afterwards. Truly Hannah's work as a "servant of all" at the clinic was a school of humility. She was learning the true meaning of the love of God, which she sought in quiet contemplation each morning. But it was *love put to the test*, in the very circumstances in which she found herself, with no room for compromise or hesitation. It would always demand all of her, as it had of Christ her master in his earthly life.

Mentally she pondered whether or not this was truly the place to which God had been leading her. *If so, where was the glory, or even the grace to endure?* she lamented. When overtaken by the pain of loneliness and near-despair, she commonly dropped onto her bed, still dressed, and simply shook, feeling as if she would fall through the mattress into an endless abyss. The "lowest place" often seemed too low to bear.

Then the Arab doorkeeper of the clinic was transferred to other work. He had been the one to let the patients in when the doctor was able to consult with them. When he left, this job fell to Hannah and took precedence over her language duties. "I would rather be a doorkeeper in the house of my God," the songwriter had said in Psalm 84:10 (NKJV). Hannah acknowledged that, in theory, there was honor in simply being included in this marvelous work for God. Still, she found her new and lower role to be beneath her sense of dignity and was humiliated at having to take it.

Every day more than one hundred poor and often illiterate men, women, and children huddled in a hallway that served as a waiting room. Upon arrival, each patient was given a number. After a short teaching service of Christian witness to these people, each number was called in turn. Waiting were distressed children, the elderly—disoriented by their pain—and couples squabbling in loud, unrestrained voices. Hannah's need to keep order constantly warred with her desire to love. She knew it was way beyond her human ability to provide the necessary atmosphere of love and healing. Thus, she learned to always turn to her Lord for help in overcoming her bitterness and acquiring the strength to alleviate others' adversity.

When the Arab was finally able to come back to his original post to relieve Hannah of the unwanted role, she was a transformed person. Again, she was *ready for anything*— even a brand-new work that God would call her to. Perhaps it would be an innovative gospel ministry on thus-far-untrod ground.

Another area of difficulty, however, existed in Hannah's life. During those first four years in Haifa, if she seldom felt *physically* strong, she also felt undernourished spiritually by the faith and practice of those around her. The spiritual dryness of the Christian fellowship threatened to diminish the courage and joy she experienced in her morning devotional times.

Hannah was used to opening up her every need and area of struggle with her former colleagues. Here, instead of experiencing the constant comfort and assurance of bringing to God every decision, she had to adjust herself to the stark reality of attending only a weekly staff prayer meeting. At those times, the adults, who were all older than she, tended to pray in careful, monotonous forms. Yes, the workers were spiritually minded and deeply devoted to their vocation; but their communion with God seemed cold and unfulfilling to Hannah's heart.

The elderly minister who led these meetings was always formally dressed and tight-lipped. Furthermore, he was highly skeptical of emotional responses or displays of feelings. He never encouraged the expression of one's personal reaction to God. Gone were any spontaneous words of praise expressed by the worshipers: "Praise be to God!" . . . fresh responses to the "inner light" . . . or anything surprising and unique coming from the preacher's mouth.

Hannah's young body and active mind found such restraint chilling and repelling to her sense of "life in Christ." What was absent, in her view, was a true heart-sharing of the ebbing, flowing dynamic of spiritual life within each soul. Of this freedom of response, meaning a sense of *dialog with her Shepherd,* she would later write with much beauty and insight in *Hinds' Feet on High Places* and other books.

Alone and unhappy in her room, she often remembered the exciting days of traveling by caravan and preaching up and down the terrain of a less hostile—though often indifferent—country. Gone was the close praying and striving together that she had shared with the members of the Friends' Evangelistic Band. Now she faced being not only uprooted from family and friends, but estranged from the customs and attitudes and habits of her own English-speaking world. She had hoped this loss would be compensated for by prayer and sharing with the other Western missionaries.

Though "by their fruit" she knew of the authenticity of the faith of her colleagues, *Hannah simply could not be like them.* Adjusting to the patterns and limitations of their style of ministry was no easy task. In fact, she felt that they put her to shame with their tireless dedication and consistency and their loving unself-consciousness.

"Their lives and service shamed me to the heart," she would later write of that time. "These new fellow workers were all miles in advance of anything I had yet attained."

Still she could not help longing for someone to pray with her—from the heart. The idea of "prayer partners," however, was sternly downplayed by their leader. He felt it was, as Hannah later remembered, "likely to lead to cliquishness and perhaps to a rather self-righteous attitude of praying that others might become a little more spiritually minded" (HH).

Hannah was self-aware enough to know her own weaknesses and, to her great credit, submitted to the wisdom of her elders. Unfortunately, she found herself in a situation of being among fellow Christians, yet as an outsider. This was not at all to her liking.

Even Sunday mornings did not offer the joy that she sought. These services rubbed her the wrong way because they were totally different from those she had known. She sat squirming through what seemed to her to be "warmed-over" sermons delivered by the old minister, who sounded almost proud to remark, "I delivered this first in 1888. . . ."

Despite the soundness and applicability of his admonitions, Hannah rebelled against their form, for she had been trained to think that "no 'stale' spiritual food should be offered, but only that which came warm and new from the heart." Much later, in her book *Kingdom of Love*, she was able to write a mature reaction to this experience:

> Love bears all that irks and burdens and disappoints us in those we are put to work with and with whom we find we disagree. And Love learns to pray for all such creatively, so that transforming power is liberated in their lives. . . .
>
> We cannot go wrong in loving. Only love is not in

word, but in deed. It does not mean saying with our lips that we do love all the true members of Christ's body, and yet acting as though we heartily disapprove of them and warning others against them. Love must express itself, and seeks for every opportunity to do so.

At this opening-up stage of ministry, what Hannah learned from such experiences was to remain with her all of her life. She was in what was to become to her *beloved* Palestine, where she uniquely served as a living testimony. But first she had to prove herself worthy of the hire. Largely due to the daily friction with those who thought, prayed, and behaved differently from her way of practicing faith, she deeply sensed that her own life and attitudes were becoming more disciplined. Nonetheless, the thought *What am I doing here?* still plagued her.

Even then, Hannah was gifted with words. Though she believed her creative expressions were from God, she struggled with how to employ them gracefully. She knew that language became stilted and ineffective when stereotyped examples were repeated. Words could also condemn *her*, especially if she called others "sinners" while denying her own shortcomings and failing to commit herself to God's transforming power. This, she felt, must come through meeting daily with the Shepherd and seeking orders only from him.

In *Hinds' Feet*, Hannah writes of the character Much-Afraid on her journey to the High Places being caught in a storm and wondering whether or not to admit defeat and turn back to safety.

Then the [Lord's] Voice spoke close at hand, "There is

a place prepared for you here beside the path. Wait there until the storm is over." In the rocky wall beside them was a little cave so low that it could be entered only if they stooped right down, and with just enough room for [Much-Afraid and her companions] to crouch inside. . . .

After they had been there for some time and the storm, far from abating, seemed to be increasing in strength . . . the whole mountain seemed to be ready to topple. Nothing was left to her but a command to offer up the promise on which she had staked her all, on the strength of which she had started on the journey.

Hannah's experience in missionary work as a medical assistant in Haifa was one of struggle and discontent, weariness and doubt, physical pain and mental anguish. It was a storm of testing, both of her initial commitment to the work and of her perseverance. It was during her early days in the clinic, in fact, that she first found out what the other staff members called her behind her back: "The proud Miss Hurnard." She had come as a daughter of privilege and wealth to do this menial work, so it was no wonder that some evidence of her "taking the lower place" shone perhaps too self-consciously in her demeanor, her manner with other workers and patients.

The workers sometimes received a break from their seemingly endless hours of service. Once, during a free hour, Hannah found herself floating in the sky-blue Mediterranean Sea, momentarily carefree and alone. Her interior thoughts were interrupted, however, as a male staff member confided (perhaps thinking he was complimenting her): "Miss Hurnard, we think that in many ways you would make an excellent *wife*. But whoever you married, *you* would have to be the boss! He'd have to do it your way, and follow your lead."

Hannah was stung. She felt herself sinking like a stone to the bottom. But in moments her sense of humor recovered, and she realized it was true! She chuckled to herself at the thought of a poor, hapless man who had somehow escaped such a life of obeying her. She might have been "the proud Miss Hurnard," but there was a twinkle in her eye and a growing sense, through this period of her life, of her human-ness and her limits.

Such a discovery made possible God's filling in her empty spaces—perhaps even the loneliness that she would experi-ence through many years of being a leader and an inde-pendent thinker in all of her work. A portion from *Hinds' Feet* reflects her thoughts on this:

> It is a terrible thing to let Pride take one by the hand, Much-Afraid suddenly discovered; his suggestions are so frightfully strong, and through the contact of touch he can press them home with almost irresist-ible force.
>
> "Come back, Much-Afraid," he urged vehemently. "Give it up before it is too late. In your heart of hearts you know that what I am saying is true and that you will be put to shame before everybody. Give it up while there is still time. Is a merely fictitious promise of living on the High Places worth the cost you are asked to pay

for it? What is it that you seek there in that mythological Kingdom above?"

Eventually, Hannah was to submit to the Voice that also said to her, reassuringly, as to Much-Afraid: "This is the way, walk ye in it" (Isa. 30:21). Here was her resting place on the path for a time: to sit through the storm of her discontent, to grow in discipline, to shed the critical spirit that had so plagued her—the self-righteousness of being intelligent, well-bred, correct, and in her case, also highly creative in the expression of her faith.

This season of "waiting out" and preparation saddened Hannah. She yearned for the lightheartedness of fellowship, the miracles of daily answered prayer, and life with like-minded servants of the King. Most of all, she probably missed the many opportunities to witness that had previously been hers during evangelistic travels. As a result, her early morning times became increasingly precious to her as the Shepherd's call to fellowship. She savored and drew from them as from a fathomless well.

> During those precious, hard-won periods, I was forced to thrust deeper and deeper into the river of his love and grace, for the sources of my spiritual life no longer lay near the surface. . . . My life seems to have taken its whole significance and pattern from those early quiet times and what I remember most clearly is a succession of radiant mornings in the secret of his presence, listening to him and then going out to try to put into practice the things he said.

Thus, the days, months, and years of endless service to complaining and sometimes ungrateful people in the clinic, growing expertise in her own evening language classes, and private times of growth in prayer and commitment to the work in Haifa continued. Then, just when she felt stretched to the limit like a rubber band about to snap, a change occurred in Hannah's orders from above.

Eight

"YOU SHALL
GO OUT WITH
JOY . . ."

Mission staff in Haifa, 1936. Hannah is standing second from the right. Dr. Churcher from the clinic is seated second from the left.

"The baby Austin," writes Ruth Laurence, "served us well! A picture of us together was taken when Hannah and I were starting on her 'vision' of putting something of God's Word into every single Jewish settlement in the land, and then later in every Arabic village as well." (Summer 1939)

(left to right) Ruth Laurence, Hannah, and Elizabeth Neatby (another coworker) outside Hill House, where they were staying for a brief holiday

In the dining room at Hill House. Hannah is in the foreground on the left; Marjorie on the right. (c. 1964)

Marjorie and Hannah outside Hannah's small cottage on Mersea Island. (1974)

Hannah Hurnard (1971)

When he putteth forth his own sheep, he goeth
before them, and the sheep follow him.

John 10:4

I find that when the Lord calls to some act of
obedience which looks absurd, or doubtful, or
even wrong, it is necessary to take the first step
in obedience without paying any attention to
doubts or fears. . . . It is hopeless to wait for
further guidance or confirmation from the
Lord until we have begun to obey in faith.

from Hearing Heart

The medical missionary staff had gathered in a circle for their weekly prayers. This time, an enthusiastic Arab evangelist had come to speak to them. Hannah was present, too, although she remained unreconciled to partaking in the usually dry and uninspiring, as it seemed to her, assembly. Surprisingly, it was during "one of *those*" meetings that Hannah was to gain certain hope about her future.

"The fields are ripe and ready for harvest," the man urged. What he meant was that none of the many villages and Jewish settlements around Haifa had had any word of the gospel brought to them as yet. He challenged the men and women in the room to take advantage of the vast opportunities for Christian witness there.

While seated and absorbing all that she heard, Hannah felt a gentle nudging within. Quietly and surely, her Lord was telling her that she was to visit every Jewish settlement in the neighborhood. She was to go from house to house, knocking on every door and offering God's Word to everyone she met, trying to speak to every person about the Lord Jesus Christ. At last, after years of waiting for God's guidance, she was being called to a form of ministry more suited to her deep desire. And it was the very thing that she had done in England and Ireland! Only now it would be in Palestine!

Simultaneously, her strong belief in these immediate, sweet secrets, whispered in love from her Lord, was challenged by a skeptical, pessimistic thought: *How impossible and foolhardy it would probably be even to attempt to use such a method in a land where most of the people were not just indifferent but hostile and antagonistic to Christ. This kind of work had never been easy in England. But in Palestine?*

"Why, many of those people to whom I believed he was now calling me to go were bound by their religious principles to spit whenever I mentioned the name of my Lord and to say, 'May the name and the memory of that blasphemer be blotted out,'" she wrote later of that time (HH).

To make the call even less likely, in this particular year (1936) Arab riots against Jews were furiously breaking out all over. Roads throughout the troubled country were laced with mines, and any and all cars were easy targets for snipers. How in the world could such a program be carried out—and by a young, relatively inexperienced woman on a war-infested trail through a hostile terrain?

Nevertheless, Hannah's thoughts and desires were only to follow her Shepherd. She would take up the task and bring Christ and peace with her on the journey to yet higher slopes of challenge and testing. "When he putteth forth his own

94

sheep, he goeth before them, and the sheep follow him"
(John 10:4).

"Thy grace is sufficient" was still the watchword.

Travel in Palestine in 1936 was extremely difficult. What
meager roads did exist were rough and largely unused; few
automobiles were available. And anyway, all local roads
washed away during the rainy season and became mere
muddy tracks. Hannah's mind reeled at the task that lay
ahead. *Even if I am able to visit a few settlements around Haifa,
passage to more distant villages is surely impossible!*

Despite the obstacles, Hannah firmly believed that what
she had clearly received was a definite call from God to *the
High Places of service.* In those regions of obedience, factors
such as overcoming the geography were certainly part of the
picture—but never the whole picture. Within herself she felt
a strength of purpose that was known to Much-Afraid at a
similar point in *her* journey: "Surely he brought me to the
heights just for this."

Yet how would she begin the ascent? Mules, donkeys,
camels—and perhaps a few horse-drawn, two-wheel carts—
had traditionally been the major means of transportation
through difficult areas, Hannah realized. But now, under the
British mandate, the scene was slowly changing.

British rule had been established sixteen years earlier, in
1920, and had brought with it the conditions for encouraging real economic growth. More money in people's hands
and new job opportunities meant that some cars had started
to appear on existing roads. But no one knew how well the
rutted former donkey trails would serve for motor vehicles.
The small British cars, which had been shipped over for use,
were fairly serviceable and efficient. Undoubtedly, traveling

to outlying posts could place drivers and their passengers in precarious situations. First, they might face open hostility, possibly even becoming caught in crossfire. Second, it would be difficult returning home safely under certain weather conditions.

The mission staff was fortunate to have recently acquired a car. Although there was nothing but a donkey trail, the doctor could now drive the nurses to the German mission clinic up on Mount Carmel. Moreover, access from Haifa to the neighboring port town of Acre was possible only by traveling up the seacoast at low tide. By that method, however, many cars would be caught in shifting sands, and thus incapacitated on the way. A road *was* being built to connect the two towns. But even with this growing accessibility, Hannah feared that there were no other workers apparently called to take to the road with her, to assist in evangelizing the towns and settlements. She felt truly alone and often frightened—but not defeated. Where would she find the courage for herself? How would she be able to persuade more of God's workers to join her in overcoming these barriers?

Hannah's proficiency in the Hebrew language had been growing steadily during her work at the clinic. Now she could converse enough to deliver the message of hope that was in her heart; she was ready to go to the people whom she had longed to reach for the Shepherd. Though Hannah bemoaned never having become fluent, her language ability, like her tongue freed of stuttering, was *sufficient for the purpose* that she was called to. She was to begin her new ministry in Jesus' own Galilee, where neither Arab nor Jewish evangelists were currently active in teaching and preaching eternal life in the Messiah, Jesus.

Every time she momentarily lost sight of the call and her heart felt as though it would drop, Hannah thought again of the High Places. Still, sometimes her mission looked not only unachievable, but unwise. Could a young woman successfully undertake such work on the strength of a prayer, a promise, and the strong will that had sustained her thus far? In her spirit, she had already silently said yes to God in this matter. But as the practical side of carrying out the work immediately faced her, she had legitimate questions. *How will I reach outlying places? Where will I stay overnight on long journeys?* Again, she turned to the source of her strength as it had always been and always would be: the quiet time with her Shepherd and the expectant wait for his answers.

She would start by taking the closest roads available, as they opened up, going as far as was feasible for day trips. These roads would lead out like a web of access to yet farther-out places as new roads were built. She decided to trust God for guidance, and, in due time, she knew the answer of where to stay would come.

But how can I face such a task alone? She would go, as she had been taught, with another woman—similar to the way Jesus had sent out his disciples "two by two." This would provide prayer and emotional support on all missions, plus a certain degree of safety.

And what about the possibility of hostility from my potential audience or even violence toward me or other missionaries? Trusting God for protection would always be a matter of faith. Surely the call itself was more important than any assurances that could be given before the fact. This was the work that Hannah had trained for in the Band, going door-to-door to present the gospel to any who would listen and respond. If she continued to follow in this way, God would take care of the safety factor, she concluded.

Another question was, Who would communicate to the Arabic people they might encounter? They were much in need of the gospel, too. For the present time, Hannah would have to leave those contacts to the growing number of Arab evangelists. She had continued to study both Hebrew and German and decided to concentrate on Jewish settlements and use her German to communicate with missionaries from that country who were also serving in Palestine.

More concerns plagued Hannah. At the time, Jewish people all over Europe were immigrating to Palestine, seeking refuge from the Nazi powers that threatened the continent. She wondered how such people, escaping from "Christian" countries where they were being violently persecuted, would ever be open *or even neutral* toward a message of Christ in the Land of Promise. As a woman facing these enormous, complicated difficulties, she wondered at the wisdom of her being sent. *Surely a man would be more effective!* she lamented.

But the call to these particular High Places was Hannah's. It was a test of her true submission and trust in her Lord. Thus, her response to such a precarious, unlikely venture had to be an echo of the prophet Isaiah's words, "Here am I, send me." Being human, of course, she felt apprehensive. To confirm her understanding of her vocation, she asked her heavenly Father to answer directly with two provisions: a car and a companion.

At this time, she was due to sail home to England for a much-anticipated visit with her aging father and his new wife, Marjorie. Marjorie Eady had been a Bible school student several years earlier when Samuel had spoken at her school. Marjorie found her vocation in assisting Samuel and offering hospitality to missionaries through the years, including her stepdaughter Hannah. Actually younger than Hannah, she would prove to be a loving friend and correspondent for the rest of Hannah's life. Hannah would later describe her as the dearest friend she had in the world.

When Hannah returned to Palestine after visiting England, she hoped to be free of her medical assistance work, which still made her feel like an "inefficient gap-filler." Yet she dreaded telling the doctor that he was about to lose the extra pair of hands she had provided in emergencies and work overloads over the past four years.

Early one morning Hannah resolutely went into the clinic to break the news to him as kindly as possible. After carefully explaining her plan, she received a surprising response. Dr. Churcher was understanding and cheerfully gave his best wishes.

"Very well," he said. "If you have received a clear call and know what God means you to do, you are free to do it. Anyway, I expect to be able to bring a fully trained nurse from England soon to help with the work here."

Hannah left his office with a lighter heart! Truly God was providing for all the details, both small and great. Two unsettled matters remained: How would God meet her specific petitions for both a car and a companion?

With the rise of Hitler and fascism in Europe, more Jewish migration than ever was rapidly altering the ethnic balance of the region. This provoked, in reaction, a nationalist Palestinian rebellion that was steadily growing in intensity. Conflict seemed inevitable. An emergency rule had just been passed declaring that no unauthorized civilians could drive on roads outside of the cities. Only authorized persons, under the utmost caution and protection, considering the warlike circumstances, were permitted to do so.

Hannah immediately went to the local authorities seeking a permit that would allow her, initially, to travel without escort on the closest local roads around Haifa. That way she would be able to take her "good news" faithfully to those nearest to where she was now positioned. At the appropriate desk she asked for the correct form. Upon handing it back, completed, to the official, she found that her intentions handily fell between the cracks of the current regulations. The baffled man stood scratching his head in amazement at her request. "Well, lady, the new regulation does not seem to have any effect on women drivers!"

Her spirit soared. She *would* be able to obey "both God and man" and to travel and speak, *as she felt compelled,* to the needy neighbors she was beginning to meet all around her. Hannah learned that when God calls an individual to a particular service, even the oddities of law and regulation can serve to make that work take root and prosper. Once she began to venture out on the roads, she found herself constantly stopped by police and military officers who were often flabbergasted, and sometimes even indignant, that a woman would be driving about unrestricted under such unpredictable and dangerous conditions. But the rule was never amended, and, fortunately, the Arabs would not knowingly attack or harm women.

Still, the threat of land mines and sniper fire was very real. Hannah prayed daily about the fact that she and any potential partners in this undertaking would be putting themselves in great peril. She knew that her own courageous—and some might think crazy—behavior could be a real problem to the British should she be kidnapped or hurt. Yet now she felt the call to be God's "wayfarer" more strongly than any desire to protect either herself or others.

Upon returning from England, Hannah brought with her a "baby" Austin car that her father had generously donated to the work—an answer to one of her two specific needs. But the perhaps greater need was for someone to appear on the scene to become her work partner. The two nurses, or "sisters," at the clinic were thrilled to see Hannah's shiny new car. Equally so, they were delighted at the prospect of using it for the purpose Hannah had in mind. Since the doctor they assisted was away for a time, they were available to help with this work. Hannah realized that the women would be ideal companions, able to provide not only Christian witness, but health care to needy families through personal "house calls." Fortunately, the clinic had kept records of all the patients who had been treated there. These people would remember the nurses and would be likely to welcome them into their homes.

On Hannah's very first day of carrying out the bold new plan, she was accompanied by Sister Caroline from Germany (or "Sister Mercy," as she would later refer to her in *Wayfarer in the Land*). The two women had decided to visit a small Jewish town not many miles away, built on the sand dunes of Haifa Bay. It was a logical place to start, in a locale where patients knew them.

There was another link to reaching the spirits of these former patients of the clinic in Haifa: All had had some taste of the regular chapel services that were conducted in the waiting room there. Hannah and Sister Caroline knew that that fact could serve as an opening to any natural spiritual curiosity. It would, as well, provide a remembered connection with their experience of healing through the doctor and nurses there.

That first day was hot and stifling, and the little sunbaked town had streets that were mere shifting sand. Annoyingly, the wayfaring witnesses' feet sank as they approached the row of patchily painted doors on the houses lined up before them. Just taking steps was a struggle! In almost every house they were allowed to enter, they would read the Bible and leave some Christian literature.

These difficult, but important, primary steps to evangelizing Palestine gave Hannah a sense of peace and accomplishment. Even though the message of Christ was not always what people *wanted* to hear, the laborers had arrived for their work.

Finally, after all the patients they knew in that first town had been seen and witnessed to without much resistance, they faced an empty, unplanned afternoon. *What if our next encounters are more antagonistic, even threatening?* Hannah pondered silently.

Between the morning and afternoon the two women stopped to eat a picnic lunch. Years later Hannah would write, "I still remember vividly the hot, smelly sand, and parched stalks sticking up here and there, thickly encrusted with dirty white snails, and how sordid and depressing it all seemed." Hannah suddenly had an awful feeling that she simply could not face the work ahead of her. "I could see that Sister Mercy felt exactly the same. When we had eaten our sandwiches, we prayed together. It seemed terribly difficult at that moment to realize the Lord's presence, but certainly he was there, for we both received the strength to get up and start the work which we still felt so unable to do" (WL).

But rushing back into her mind came the memory of what God had already done so miraculously in her life: He had *rescued* her from the painful despair of doubt, *healed* her of her handicaps, and *empowered* her to make her his messenger. Now he had led her to this place of beginning to practice, at last, the very work for which she felt most suited—and in which her heart delighted.

In *Hinds' Feet*, she would later write:

> "You, my Lord, never regarded me as I actually was, lame and weak and crooked and cowardly. You saw me as I would be when you had done what you promised and had brought me to the High Places, when it could be truly said, 'There is none that walks with such a queenly ease, nor with such grace, as she.'
>
> "You always treated me with the same love and graciousness as though I were a queen already and not wretched little Much-Afraid." Then she looked up into his face and for a time could say no more, but at last she added, "My Lord, I cannot tell you how greatly I want to regard others in the same way."

This was the key: to love and serve others as her Shepherd had loved and guided her to this very place.

To God, in his will, it was as though this "impossible" task was already accomplished. The women decided that they *could* do it—in his power.

They drove back to town slowly, discussing how to begin. And feeling still very weak and foolish and hopelessly inadequate in themselves, they chose to begin at the very first house on the very first street they reached.

Hannah tapped on the door—and not a single word she could possibly say came to her mind in that instant. Suddenly, the door opened. A man stared out at them and their bags of books and then closed the door on them quickly, saying in Hebrew that he didn't wish to buy anything. Though discouraged, they pressed on. Surely this was wasted effort at best, if not agonizing failure. Where was God's presence to show them the way? They wanted to know.

The second house was that of a cobbler, and the cobbler himself, a little hunchbacked, slightly disheveled man, was sitting working in the doorway of his home-shop. He glanced up, surprised at such visitors. But then Sister Caroline, with her kindly, ruddy face, smiled at him and held out to him the gift of a small New Testament. Suddenly he began to smile with delight, raised himself up, and motioned to them to sit down on a bench.

"I have met you before," he said excitedly to Sister Caroline.

Years before, he told them, he had been a patient at a hospital in a large German city where Sister Caroline had worked. He was one who had always wanted to hear the gospel but had never been offered a chance. Sister Caroline was now able to share the Good News in her own German language with the man. They handed him all of the pamphlets and booklets they could spare. At their departure, he stood at the door motioning widely with his hands.

"You must come again!" he implored.

How weak had been our faith precisely moments before, Hannah remembered. Could she dare to imagine the people of Palestine, to whom she would minister, as *needy* just as she had once been? Could she see them as perhaps *seeking*, also, as she had sought the Shepherd of her life? She commented to Sister Caroline, "It was just like our Father's love and care to lead us to that particular house, and let us glimpse so early something of the possibilities and opportunities before us."

The two women visited several other houses that day and, at one point, were actually invited inside by a middle-aged woman who also spoke German. Sister Caroline, made bold by the success with the cobbler, smiled and asked if she might have the privilege of giving the woman something to read. They read and talked for some time, and she made a new friend. Again, God had opened the way.

When they finally turned to drive home at the end of that extraordinary and pivotal day, joy filled their hearts to overflowing. "No matter how depressing and discouraging the visiting might have seemed at the time, whenever we sat down to rest afterwards, or turned our faces homeward, the Great Shepherd always gave us this peculiarly radiant joy," Hannah later recalled (WL).

She continued the pattern of visiting, going sometimes with the other nurse, Sister Ida Dreitschman, a Jewish Christian from Romania ("Sister Patience" in *Wayfarer in the Land*). Then, after a few weeks, the doctor returned, and the sisters were no longer able to travel with Hannah. Exactly at the same time, a young Hebrew woman named Frieda Zeiden offered to be Hannah's partner for the work. Since she knew both Hebrew and German, the two main languages spoken, she was the ideal person to share Hannah's vision. Together the two developed a style of great harmony. Frieda, or "Peace" as Hannah calls her, was able to do the preaching. She was a convert herself and was filled with fervor for the task. Having experienced much reproach and misunderstanding from family and friends, she had a boldness and joy, coupled with a deep understanding of those to whom she ministered.

Like Jesus, her Lord, the gentle but formidable Frieda was able to adapt her message to the particular needs of each person she encountered; or, as the apostle Paul said, "to be all things to all people" so that she might win some. She seemed intuitively to understand the spiritual condition of each person and was able to offer what was most needed at the moment.

Amazing stories of Hannah's experiences of witnessing door-to-door, village to village, throughout the Holy Land, are recorded in her book *Wayfarer in the Land*. Jesus' steps also became her steps. In other words, she had come to identify closely with her Lord who, in his ministry, had encountered both open hearts and hostility toward the things of his kingdom. Hannah's sacrificial work among Jewish settlements continued in this way over a period of two years with the help of various partners that God provided. One of these was Ruth Laurence ("Faith," in *Wayfarer in the Land*). She once wrote these remembrances of "a visiting day with Hannah":

The day before, Hannah and I met for prayer. Spread out before us were our maps of Israel and lists of all the settlements from the Jewish agency. We prayed over the district we were working in, the places visited and those still to visit. Then we'd plan our next day's route to two more villages.

In the morning, we would load the car with Scripture booklets, gospels, and tracts in many different languages, for Jews were pouring in from so many countries. Reaching the chosen village, we would go from door to door. We had told of the Bible shop in Haifa where a Bible in their own language could be bought, and we had offered our booklets.

The men were all out working, and children were at school, so we mostly met mothers and toddlers. The reception varied but was usually friendly. For the toddlers, our friends [who supported us for this work] had sent us used English stamp books turned into tiny scrapbooks of pretty little pictures. How often producing one from our pockets had opened the way, with a less responsive mother, for us to leave something for herself and her husband also!

At midday we would eat our sandwiches, often in some beauty spot where we could quickly gather some glorious wild flowers to take home, and then go on to a second village—after we had prayed.

On our drives we may have passed a gang of workmen who, when we stopped, crowded around to receive a booklet. So many could not cope well with the Hebrew language and were hungry to hear or read in their own familiar tongue.

107

When we reached home we thanked God for supply-
ing our every need, and prayed especially for individuals
we had talked to that day. How we wondered if and
when we could visit them again! Meanwhile, we would
pray, "May God's own Word speak and point them to
their Messiah Jesus."

I shall always thank God for Hannah's friendship and
the inspiration of working with her.

Hannah fully immersed herself in the daily realities of
ministry for which she had ached during years of patience
and preparation in the clinic.

"Ye shall go out with joy, and be led forth with peace,"
God had promised Hannah from Isaiah 55:12. And, indeed,
she and her fellow workers found this to be true. Traveling
down highly questionable roads in the baby Austin, they
sometimes came to places where the road had just been
blown up by terrorists. Or they passed through an area
where sniper fire had barely ceased. The group never took
anything for granted. Once a woman friend of Hannah's,
upon returning from a church service, was brutally shot to
death.

The rigorous routine of Hannah's ministry took its toll
on her, and in 1938 she was hospitalized due to exhaustion.
It was during this convalescence that Hannah received the
second part of her specific call to Palestine. Again, against
all reason, she felt God leading her *also* to take his truth to
every *Arab* village in the land. This seemed truly absurd, as
she knew no Arabic! And there were at least three times as
many Arab villages as there were Jewish settlements. De-

spite her objections, she found herself deeply convicted again. She would later recall,

> As I looked out over the land, I saw out in the deserts, and in the hidden valleys between the mountains, un-numbered tents belonging to wandering tribes who had no settled villages. And as I stared and stared, sick at heart, I heard my Lord say, "Why do you never pray for all those places, Grace? Who is carrying my message to them? Is the water of life not meant for all these villages too? . . . Now I want you to claim every place in the land, every single village, and every single encamp-ment. . . . Are you ready to go with me?" (WL)

She hardly felt strong enough. In a few weeks she was to leave for a further rest in England. Yet surprisingly, when her own doctor from Haifa came to visit her, he did not laugh at his patient's attempt to carry out such a plan. Amazingly, he said, "Well, you will just have time to make a start before you leave for England, and then it will be easier for you to launch out steadily on your return."

To carry out her new work, Hannah acknowledged that she had to rely on a more seasoned woman missionary ("Miss Piety" in *Wayfarer in the Land*) who had begun such a minis-try twenty years earlier, but now had had to cut back her visits to Arab villages because of the warlike conflict. With Hannah's support and enthusiasm, she was willing to take up the call again. The two began by visiting a village about twenty miles away.

Hannah was later to reflect that it was a good thing they did not know at that stage what they discovered after arrival at their destination: "The village we had chosen had just gotten itself into serious trouble for harboring and supporting the leader of an Arab terrorist gang who had been raiding other villages for supplies. The gang had been allowed to store their arms in this village and the rebel chief made his headquarters there! An armed force had been sent to clear the district of these rebels. . . . As it happened, however, the police force left an hour or two before our arrival" (WL).

Into such a powder keg of potential violence came the gentle women with the Word from their loving Lord. Miss Piety delivered her sermon in a large, dark, smoke-grimed room with two small windows. The men and children who came sat on the stone floor spread with rush mats. There was no furniture, only a charcoal brazier and implements for brewing coffee.

"I realized," Hannah wrote later of her fears that night, "that if they became angry, escape was impossible." Miss Piety's appearance, however, was reassuring. Her face was beaming with joy and friendliness. "The whole roomful of people realized this at once, and responded . . . to the love and earnestness with which she preached to them. There was no trace of hostility or resentment, and the message was listened to with quiet attention." *How could the Lord have let them start the work again under such conditions?* they had wondered at first.

"But we felt afterwards that he had definitely permitted it as the seal we had asked for, for we were never likely to find ourselves visiting a more dangerous hotbed of anger and anti-British feeling." Truly, anyone known to have connections with any British agency, including missionary societies, was at risk in those perilous days.

Though it took her a long time to get accustomed to the

squalor and dirt of many of the places they were entertained in, Hannah did feel the beginning of the strange fascination and affection that made the visiting of those Arab villages the greatest joy and pleasure of her life.

Thus, Hannah became, as she called herself, "God's chauffeur," driving freely to take the Good News to both Jewish and Arab settlements. She continued without interruption, even through the further restrictions of travel that were enforced during World War II when, for eight years, it was impossible to leave the country.

After Hannah's vision had been expanded to send her to Moslem as well as Jewish settlements, she went out in her Austin one time, taking with her a particularly frail missionary. The terrain was filled with huge boulders—so obtrusive that men had to stop and push the women in their car over the rocks to keep them going. Later, on the missionaries' successful return, they were stopped by a British policeman who asked them where they had been. When they gave him the name of the village, he stepped back in astonishment.

"Surely not!" he exclaimed. "We had to take our strongest armored car there a day or two ago, and we broke a back axle on those rocks and were stranded for hours before we could get towed back!"

In such experiences of faith, Hannah risked all to bring word of Christ to a people who were openly hostile to all that he represents and often highly suspicious of those who followed him. But that is only part of the story. Once, when visiting a highly orthodox Jewish village, an old man took her gift of a Hebrew New Testament gratefully and said, "For many years I have wanted to read this book, but never found

111

a copy." Hannah found open doors for the gospel in villages everywhere she went.

Looking back, Hannah realized the care and timing that had made all of this possible. In 1947 came the announcement that Britain intended to withdraw from Palestine on May 14, 1948, and transfer responsibility for the region to the United Nations. Then, after the United Nations attempted to partition Palestine into separate Arab and Jewish states, rebellion broke out. Due to the Arab-Jewish conflict that ensued, scores (perhaps hundreds) of the same Arab villages that Hannah and Miss Piety had reached became deserted ruins. Their inhabitants became refugees in neighboring Moslem countries. Had the servants waited, opportunity would have vanished like the shifting sand of the village streets.

"Then we understood why God had set the door of opportunity so wide open, and held it open, so that no one was able to shut it. It was his purpose that every place should have the opportunity of hearing the gospel before the fire of war swept through the land and hundreds of thousands of its inhabitants were scattered."

Miraculous events had certainly occurred to the same young woman who had once been a stuttering, fearful teenager, kneeling terrified in a little room at Keswick in 1924. Now happy and fulfilled, Hannah was beginning to feel more akin to "Grace and Glory" in *Hinds' Feet*, whose feet had become like the hinds', leaping on the mountain places in love and witness.

> How lovely and how nimble are thy feet,
>   O prince's daughter!

They flash and sparkle and can run more fleet
    Than running water.
On all the mountains there is no gazelle,
    No roe or hind,
    Can overtake thee nor can leap as well—
But lag behind.

Nine

LOVE PLANS THE WAY

Some task thou may'st set me,
Quick or hard to fret me,
Let my heart unswerving,
Trust thee and obey.
Out of present sorrow
Springs a gladder morrow,
Love that bled to save me,
Love plans all my way.

from Hearing Heart

Faithful is he that calleth you, who also will do it.

1 Thessalonians 5:24

L *ord, dare we continue this work?* Hannah prayed fervently. It was 1946, and the situation in Palestine had become more and more unsafe.

Hannah, now forty-one, had been working tirelessly among Jewish and Arab people for ten years—right through World War II, during which she and other foreign missionaries and workers in the country were unable to leave. For eight years Hannah had been prevented from visiting her beloved England. Yet she gave special thanks for the little car that had enabled her to labor as "God's chauffeur." It had been shipped to the country just before it would have become impossible to do so!

Although officially, during this troubled time, no cars were allowed to travel about except with an armed convoy—or special VIP permits—Hannah continued driving unescorted all over the country.

Many times she and her partners were threatened and frightened by the violence around them. They learned that one other woman, a government social worker who had also driven around freely, ended up being killed by stray bullets. Not once, however, were the missionaries ever attacked or prevented from preaching the gospel. Sometimes, when they spoke openly in public places, they knew that Arab terrorists were watching. But even *they* could not hinder that particular, ongoing work of God.

During the Arab-Israeli conflict, it was almost impossible to get spare parts for cars. By now, Hannah's car was decrepit. By December she hardly ventured out at all except on well-traveled highways, as the little Austin had become so unreliable. Replacement tires were unobtainable. Unless a car was guarded all night while parked on the street, its parts would be stolen and sold on the black market.

With her travels so restricted, Hannah turned her attention to training a group of young Armenian and Arab Christians, whom she hoped would form an evangelistic band to carry on the work. One morning she was to drive her friends to a monthly prayer meeting in connection with this ministry. Before they left on the precarious journey, though it was not a long trip, Hannah warned her colleagues, "Please do sit down very gently. The back axle broke the other day, and though it has been patched up it may go again at the least jar. And my spare wheel either fell off or was taken off while we were out visiting last week, so if we have a puncture on the way, we shall just be stranded."

The others sighed and steeled themselves. They all were used to hearing from Hannah these dismal realities of the risks of travel. But that morning as she drove them toward

Bethlehem, it was as though she were steering a carton of eggs on wheels. One worker felt led to make a comment.

"You know, I feel the time has come when we really must ask God to give Hannah another car!"

Hannah was taken aback. Why, she hadn't even thought of that—it seemed so preposterous to ask for such a thing in war time.

"I . . . don't know," she answered hesitantly. "Think of the tremendous cost—more than twice as much as before the war . . . and the waiting list is about two years . . . and then we wouldn't be given priority, as would the government officials or doctors. . . ."

Yet God has promised to supply our every need, she thought prayerfully.

When the group finally agreed that this was what they should pray for, they also acted. They went to the English Morris Car agency and inquired as to their chances of getting a new car. Carefully removing his eyeglasses, the agent looked hard at the unusual group of ardent workers and said, "None at all, I'm afraid."

But then, brightly, in his best salesman's "good news" voice, he offered a suggestion. "However, if you care to buy a Morris 8 van, we have two, and it isn't necessary to obtain a permit for a commercial van."

What a laugh! thought Hannah. *What would I do with such a large vehicle?* Meanwhile the man, who had been informed of their intended purpose, went on with a most convincing sales pitch.

"You might find a van very convenient for your work, Miss Hurnard. They are built high off the ground and are particularly practical on hard, rocky tracks. You do not need anything upholstered or chrome plated on such rough journeys as you undertake. And, moreover, they are much cheaper than a sedan or anything else. It is true they have only two seats, but if you wish, you can have another put in the back. I can show you one now. . . ."

And so the little group became sold on "Plan B" for transportation. They would continue the work, as it turned out, in more safety and efficiency than the use of any car could have afforded. A few additions were made to the van: a third seat, a compartment to hold literature, and another for food goods. The dealer would even take the baby Austin as a trade-in!

Eager to reach Moslem villages as well, and with a new van that would have made it all possible, Hannah was unprepared for the next test of her faith.

Terrorist activities of the warring factions in the country had worsened since the first formal Arab rebellion ten years earlier, in 1936. As early as 1937 the British government had considered partitioning Palestine into separate Jewish and Arab states after deciding its obligations to the two peoples were mutually irreconcilable. However, upon further study, partition was deemed impractical in 1938 and was not pursued. The Arabs, by far the majority of Palestinian residents, were strongly opposed to giving up part of their country to Jews. And with the influx of thousands of Jews fleeing persecution before and during World War II, tensions between the two factions had continued to mount.

Now, in 1946, a series of uprisings broke out in which terrorists took British people captive. Some hostages were being held for ransom. Once, during a full court session, a judge was abducted. The taking of prisoners was intended to force the British government to meet terrorist demands and eventually to end the mandate itself.

The growing precariousness of daily life led the mandatory government in Palestine to pass an evacuation edict on January 1, 1947: All British women and children were to be transferred to safer locales within *three days*. Only the British military forces were able to remain in order to try to quash the rebel activities in both the Arab and Jewish sectors of the country. This evacuation, labeled "Operation Polly" by the British, came to be known instead as "Operation Folly," due to the number of disrupted lives, the panic, and the fear that it created.

Hannah bore the disruption gracefully, even though, for the vast majority of doubtful women and bewildered and frightened children, it was an extremely difficult time. Thus, Hannah embarked on a literal "flight to Egypt" to escape the dangers that had overtaken her world and its familiar terrain.

Surely this timing is a mistake! Hannah moaned inwardly. It seemed as though the setback was a pure contradiction of the assurance she had that the work must go on. Riding in the small airplane that shuttled passengers to larger aircraft, she suffered from claustrophobia, knowing that she had no means of escape and a terrible fear of heights. On the other hand, she found God's presence to be real and comfortably reassuring as she endured the physical discomfort of the trip and the disruption of her work that it represented. She would later write of the experience in *Hearing Heart*:

> All the promises did indeed seem contradicted, and God had not intervened to prevent our being driven forth from our "land of promise," but he still remained

faithful. He would bring us back in his own good time—and I left my precious six-weeks-old van behind me as a surety and a pledge of his promise. Even in this, God was ever doing "a new thing."

Thankfully, the evacuation proceeded without incident. The passengers disembarked and went by motorcade to Maadi Camp in Egypt, where they were to stay in dormitories. After a few weeks Hannah was able to go back to England by ship. There she would visit her father and her stepmother.

A multitude of questions filled Hannah's mind during this period. *Why has God taken me from the mission field where I belong? Are there yet other "high places" to which I shall go, albeit hesitantly at first, and then in confidence of my God's leading and guidance all along? Will I be called to return to Palestine? Or is 1932–1947, fulfilling as it has been, to stand as my career in this kind of service?*

After enjoying four months of rest and recovery from her rigorous travel and years of strenuous work and deprivation, Hannah received a letter from CMJ, the mission with which she had been working in Palestine. The letter had been sent out to supporters to request prayer for the ongoing work in Palestine.

She learned that the medical staff associated with the mission had been allowed to remain in the Jerusalem Mission Hospital. However, the workers found themselves in a curious position. While they were in a Jewish sector of the city, and most of the people were Jews, quite a number of the hospital nurses were Arab. The tension between these two peoples in the land had accelerated to the point that the

Arab nurses and housekeeper were being forced to leave the employ of the mission hospital as soon as suitable replacements could be found. Yet it seemed impossible to fill these positions with Jewish workers because of their intense anger against Great Britain and all that it stood for. Even though individual Britons sympathized with Jewish efforts, from 1939 on British official policy supported Arab interests. Even Christian missionaries were at risk. The greatest need the hospital had was for a housekeeper to come at once.

Hannah read the mission's plea to a friend in England who was joining her in prayer over the situation. "Whoever they get to become housekeeper is someone who will not have it easy—and who will need much prayer support," she commented. She was well aware of the danger of being an active Christian in that land, now that the violence was so rampant. Christians were hated for being British, as well as for being Christian.

So Hannah prayed, "Lord, please give the special person who will take on this task an extra share of your love and grace, which she will need to take this on at all." Little did she know how personally God would answer that prayer.

The next day Hannah received a personal letter from CMJ containing a shocking request: Would she agree to return to Jerusalem and take on the task of the much-needed housekeeper? "We do expect that we shall be able to gain necessary government permission," they wrote, "as hospital provisions are so vital in such a time of turmoil and need."

"Me—a housekeeper for a hospital?" Hannah was incredulous. She had never been much good at household tasks even in her personal life, and the thought of taking on administrative responsibility for a whole hospital was preposterous. "All I can cook is a piece of toast! How could I even know what food provisions are needed—much less quantities, and preparation, and servicing a kitchen . . . ?" Hannah's head was swimming with the ironies of being asked to be someone she simply was not. *Surely God is making a mistake in calling me. Yet . . . I do speak both Hebrew and Arabic and have had extensive experience with both groups in my witnessing and meeting people throughout the country during the last eleven years.*

Yet . . . I have a deep understanding of the situation in that country, as well as how it has evolved, and I believe I could show compassion (as my Lord has to me) to people on both sides of the issues.

Yet . . . my name has been put forward, and I have been called the only person who can take on such a task among both groups at this time.

Her mind reeled as the evidence began to overwhelm her.

I will write and tell them I simply can't cook or organize. They must find someone else, she decided. At her friend's prodding, they prayed specifically for the person who would fill the position. And Hannah's heart was touched with a desire to do what was right.

After several sleepless nights, she felt compelled to write back with a gracious thankfulness for being considered and declared her willingness to go *if it was God's will.* But she was careful to admit her shortcomings in just these kinds of work. Then there was nothing to do but await God's leading in the matter.

A response from the mission committee came back almost immediately. Hannah's heart nearly stopped when she read the letter. They were asking her to come! Since the staff had already been trained by the present housekeeper, she was needed in a largely advisory capacity to listen and help. She would carry out policies already established and drive in her own van, which had been left parked on the hospital compound when she had had to leave so suddenly.

Hannah sought her father's opinion on the matter. Although even *he* had doubted the wisdom of this call, he supported her.

And then the joy came. . . . Hannah felt the assurance that it was always safe to put her hand in the hand of the living Lord and to go with him anywhere he called. So, in the same year as the evacuation, 1947, this unquestionably needed, solitary British woman was being called back to Palestine to serve again, despite the dangers and arguments against such a move.

Hannah left her home and family in Colchester, England. It had been a farewell visit unawares, for it was the last time she was ever to see her beloved father. Thankfully, she went back with his blessing. He had said that he was very proud of her brave work. In her father's eyes was mirrored the respect and care she knew would follow her back to her mission. Hannah also rejoiced that she was able to fulfill what her mother had so hoped for in her daughter and had expressed on her deathbed years before: "Hannah will take over for me. . . ."

When Hannah arrived in Jerusalem, she was given kind and courteous help by the retiring housekeeper for several weeks. Then she was on her own. "On the very day that she left and the keys were handed over to me," Hannah would later recall, "partition was announced [by the United Nations], and the Jews and Arabs began the last desperate phase of their long struggle. Great Britain then declared their intention of giving up the mandate within six months" (HH).

It was on November 29, 1947, that the United Nations General Assembly adopted recommendations to partition the country into separate Arab and Jewish states, which would retain an economic union. The announcement met with strong Arab opposition and sparked civil war throughout Palestine.

Hannah later wrote of this time:

> Then it began to become clear to me in the most extraordinary way why God had called me to accept the hospital job just at that identical moment. . . .
>
> From the very first day that I took over the housekeeping, I had, personally, to fetch in my precious God-given van every crumb of food that we ate. The hospital itself did not possess a car, but I went daily in my commercial van out of the Jewish into the Arab area in order to buy all our supplies. This was only possible because I was a Britisher and so was granted permission to pass through the British Zone which acted as a sort of buffer state between the two belligerent areas. (HH)

Life in Jerusalem remained threatening and difficult. Since the patients at the hospital were poor Palestinian Arabs and Jews without other means of medical care, there was much temptation for them to steal what they could not buy outside the medical center—not even on the black market. Every item was valuable: linens, and small equipment such as thermometers, bandages, nightgowns. And the hospital could only replace such items by buying them back from the black market—to which the patients probably would have sold them in the first place!

So in the interest of effective, ongoing medical work, one of Hannah's tasks was to "frisk" patients as they departed, by running her hands down their back and front, to discover any small linen stuck in pockets, or metal items jangling together in a wide sleeve. What a variety of things she recovered! Reaching and searching, she looked for all the world, at times, like a magician pulling out handkerchiefs from nowhere before the watching staff! However, in Hannah's eyes, it was sad to have to be a policewoman in this way. Even children had been recruited to do the dirty work. *Yet I can see how much I am needed here,* she acknowledged.

And she began to understand further why she had been assigned to this new stage of ministry in Palestine. It was because of her housekeeping work that she had permission to continue to buy precious gasoline for running errands. In one instance, just before the partitioning, she had to transport the Arab workers at the hospital out of the Jewish district. It was by God's grace that this was accomplished without incident.

During this period of upheaval, there was no communication or interchange between the two warring factions. It was hoped that the removal of the British mandate would leave the highly tense and dangerous situation for the people to work out between them. This proved impossible because of the deep hostility of these two peoples toward each other, which dates from biblical times. In fact, conflict over these issues was to continue for the next forty-five years. Even the long-awaited and historic peace agreement between the Palestinian Liberation Organization (PLO) and Israel in September 1993 did not fulfill the hopes and expectations many had for it.

Yet at that time the fighting escalated further, and around mid-January of 1948 it became clear that the hospital would have to close down. Some of the English hospital staff had departed already. Any Arab workers living and working in the vicinity were in constant jeopardy. Only three members of the mission team were to remain: the Reverend Ronald Adeney, chaplain; Ruth Clark, the headmistress of the CMJ Girls' School in Jerusalem; and Hannah. The two women were living on the upper floor of the mission doctor's house. On the lower level, about forty young Jewish girls came daily to school, when conditions permitted.

Hannah's work then was, incredibly, to drive back and forth through the British military zone, taking workers to the mission hostel in Arab territory. From there they were taken by armed escorts to the airports to fly back to safety in England.

By spring 1948 it had become clear that Jerusalem would be left in a state of siege once the British military withdrew on May 14. Arab forces surrounded the city. Not just Palestinian Arabs, but those from neighboring Arab countries had been enlisted for this effort as well.

Hannah's Morris 8 van was also to be used in "Operation Mercy" on May 1, 1948. This was a plan by which Hebrew Christians in Jerusalem were evacuated and taken to Haifa, where they would join other Hebrew Christians from around the country to sail for England and safety. As the battle for Jerusalem intensified and food and safety became more difficult to secure, it seemed advisable to CMS and other mission boards that these Hebrew Christians desiring to leave be transported out.

Several other available civilian vehicles, besides Hannah's van, were eventually aided by two army pickup trucks in order to allow thirty-five Hebrew Christians and four English nuns to escape. Hannah remained to serve. Author Kelvin Crombie writes of her courage in his book, *For the Love of Zion*:

> Early in the morning of 14 May, Miss Hurnard drove down to the Old City [of Jerusalem] to do her customary shopping. The British officer told her that the British forces would withdraw from the zone outside Jaffa Gate at 8:30 a.m., and that there would no doubt be a scramble between the Jewish and Arab forces to seize these positions. She did her shopping and made it back to the hospital. This was her last excursion to the Old City.[*]

Later, Hannah wrote of that memorable time. "When I reached the Hospital, the ambulances were already bringing in the Jewish dead and wounded . . ." (WW). This was the day before the new state of Israel came to birth.

By May 14, all movement was halted out of this enclosed and blockaded area. Absolutely no communication with other Jewish areas was possible. Armies, land mines, and bombshells made travel impossible.

Anti-British sentiment was fierce. Early in February the offices of the English newspaper, the *Palestine Post*, had been bombed. The force of that explosion was sufficient to shatter

*Kelvin Crombie, *For the Love of Zion* (London: Hodder & Stoughton, 1991), 222.

sixteen windows of the hospital, half a mile away! The nearby offices of the Magen David Adom, which was a Jewish "Red Cross" agency, had also been damaged as a result of the blast. And so CMJ had the opportunity to hand over its outpatient clinic to the Red Cross.

The Jewish authorities took over the mission hospital itself, which was gladly given to them during the crisis, rent-free for one year. The Jewish hospital, which was outside the area, had been cut off by Arab lines.

All water pipelines to the city had been cut off by the Arabs. American and British workers left the city; so did the English "sisters." None of them wanted to endure such restrictions on their ministries. When their houses and buildings were vacated, they were immediately taken over by the Jews. Most of these homes had their own cisterns, which the occupants hoped would not run dry before the rainy season replenished them. Hannah and her two coworkers confined themselves to the doctor's house on the grounds throughout the siege. Having their own cistern and pump, they did not have to venture far. The pump, however, was outside, and Chaplain Adeney was nearly caught by mortar fragments on one occasion.

That summer, 1948, bombs, shells, and shrapnel falling on the helpless city made it seem as though earthquakes were taking place continuously. Mount Zion stood covered in smoke as had the Mount of the Law in the Old Testament days of Moses. Numbers of people were killed daily.

Since there were no burial areas in the besieged part of the city, bodies had to be taken out at night and piled up in caves that were on the outskirts, just within the limits of the campaign. Later they would be taken to a mass grave.

At night Hannah would pray, *Lord, have mercy,* and try to sleep on a small mattress in the basement. Her colleagues, Ruth Clark and Ronald Adeney, would pray and watch nearby. Then for a few hours, Hannah would watch while one of the others slept. Sirens wailed and the city itself seemed to shake uncontrollably about them. Yet none of them doubted the God who had called them to this pivotal moment in human and biblically prophetic history.

Even in this time of war, Hannah was aware of strange and beautiful gifts bestowed by her Creator amid the dangers: a sudden flock of pigeons overhead, fig trees budding, red and pink hibiscus blossoms, the cool Mediterranean Sea air. Finding spiritual and emotional consolation in nature, as she always had as a child, it was still possible for her to whisper, "Thank you, Lord." She learned to worship her heavenly Father and enjoy the fellowship of Christ in the beauty of his holiness, even in this extremity. Like so many other steadfast saints, she humbly prayed in the midst of danger.

Is this part of your purpose for me? Hannah knew she had been brought to this very place to minister to Jesus' own people. Now she could not help but identify with her Lord's lament: "When he beheld the city, [Jesus] wept over it" (Luke 19:41). Softly, behind the sounds of women wailing over their loved ones in the hospital garden, she could hear her Shepherd's comforting words, *"Now thou shalt see what I will do."*

These rich experiences—of ministry and service to the most needy, of survival through a world war—were to give rise to the depth of Hannah's spiritual understanding. And they were to spur her on to the challenge to "write the things which you have seen" and heard and learned (Rev. 1:19,

NKJV). The initial writings that led to her two books *Hearing Heart* and *Wayfarer in the Land* were accomplished at that time.

In her personal journal, published by CMJ as *Watchmen on the Walls*, Hannah penned her reaction to what she witnessed that year in Jerusalem:

> Surely 1948 has been one of the most momentous years in the history of the world, perhaps the most momentous since that amazing time when God Himself appeared upon the earth in the form of a man. . . . In this amazing year of 1948, another God-planned and prophet-foretold wonder has taken place—the rebirth of the unchanging, undying, unassimilated Jewish nation. . . . On May 15th, as the new State of Israel was proclaimed, the British Mandate ended, and as Israel again became a nation in the land of Israel, the thirty-seventh chapter of Ezekiel was read in Hebrew over the radio—the glorious prophecy of the scattered dry bones which were suddenly joined together with flesh and sinews, and then received the life of God. We who remained in the country while the astonishing miracle happened will never forget with what a noise and shaking those bones came together. . . .

The fighting, of course, was far from over. Hannah further noted:

> The "Time of Jacob's Trouble" cannot come to an end, until Jacob becomes Israel in very truth, by worshipping and obeying Israel's God, and acknowledging their Messiah and Saviour. . . . Partition can never be called full

possession, and full possession, the Scriptures seem to show clearly, will depend upon their own attitude and actions in the Land.

Eventually the siege was over, and food, mail, and supplies were able to be delivered again. Hannah commented, "Naturally we three British citizens, remaining almost as enemy aliens in the country, found this a strange time." By July 1949 a UN mediator had secured armistice agreements between Israel and most of its neighbors.

During this troubled time, Hannah received word from England of her father's serious illness. Her stepmother, Marjorie, urged her to come home at once. Hannah did so, but due to transportation delays and difficulties, she did not arrive soon enough to speak to her father one last time. Her feelings of loss were partly eased by the joyful confidence that her earthly father was in the place prepared for him in their heavenly Father's realm. There was also comfort in knowing she would someday be reunited with him there. Hannah stayed long enough to assist in the preparations and attend the services of the funeral and burial.

The Lord graciously allowed Hannah a much-needed vacation following her return trip to Israel. She experienced rest and spiritual renewal on the island of Cyprus. With her went fond memories of "the old home in which I had been born and where I had been welcomed back by my father on all my furloughs from missionary work in the Middle East" (LL).

Reentering the newly established state of Israel, Hannah and her partners no longer needed permission to stay there, nor permits to continue their work. Within a few weeks the missionary team's evangelism efforts, which had been merely *postponed* in God's providence, were able to be resumed. In Hannah's own words:

> It was the first time since the destruction of Jerusalem in A.D. 70 and the dispersion of the Jewish nation over the then-known world that it had been possible to witness to the Lord Jesus in every place in the country. (TSR)

By God's amazing grace and enabling power, her work had been accomplished among these diverse peoples during the eleven years between 1936 and 1947—right through World War II. In many ways, Hannah Hurnard's own story to this point fits the pattern of spiritual growth that she describes in *Hinds' Feet*. That allegory tells how God worked in one life to help bring about the miraculous.

"Faithful is he that calleth you, who also will do it." "I have led thee in right paths." These were the promises given to this trustworthy, tested, and proven servant of her Lord. Love himself had planned and been Hannah's guide through it all. As she wrote in *Hinds' Feet*:

> The floods can never drown thy Love,
> Nor weaken thy desire,
> The rains may deluge from above
> But never quench thy fire.
> Make soft my heart in thy strong flame,
> To take the imprint of thy Name.

This was, indeed, what had happened to the former Miss Much-Afraid—she had received the new name of Grace and Glory. In *Hinds' Feet,* the Shepherd describes the transformation this way: "You have learned well, Grace and Glory. Now I will add one thing more. It was these lessons which you have learned which enabled me to change the crippled Much-Afraid into Grace and Glory with the hinds' feet. Now you are able to run, leaping on the mountain and able to follow me wherever I go, so that we need never be parted again."

However, Hannah's life beyond Israel, she would discover, was to reveal even more unexpected turns and surprising twists.

Ten

SONG
OF THE
SHEPHERD

"It is quite true that the way up to the High Places is both difficult and dangerous," said the Shepherd. "It has to be, so that nothing which is an enemy of Love can make the ascent and invade the Kingdom. Nothing blemished or in any way imperfect is allowed there, and the inhabitants of the High Places do need hinds' feet. I have them Myself," He added with a smile, "and like a young hart or a roebuck I can go leaping on the mountains and skipping on the hills with the greatest ease and pleasure. But, Much-Afraid, I could make yours like hinds' feet also, and set you upon the High Places. You could serve Me then much more fully and be out of reach of all your enemies. I am delighted to hear that you have been longing to go there, for, as I said before, I have been waiting for you to make the suggestion."

from Hinds' Feet on High Places

What path shall I go in next? Hannah had been asking her Lord fervently. Now that statehood was established in the land of Palestine, she sensed that the shape of her ministry was gradually changing.

After another trip to England to take care of her father's estate, she was en route to Israel when she stopped to take a three-week break—which included her forty-fourth birthday—in awe-inspiring Braunwald, Switzerland. Hannah especially loved to visit the Swiss Alps, where she had first seen

139

and been enraptured by the "High Places" during her youth. *Twenty-seven years ago, Mother was here with me on her last holiday in this place*, Hannah remembered. In her journal, she wrote:

> Now I am sitting on a huge green slope, starred with tiny blue gentians, and the buttercups are scattered like gold all around me. This is the Braunwald Alp, and the snow mountains rise like walls on three sides of it. I sit here and look out on beauty beyond expression. To the right is an immense cliff over which the Brumbach waterfall leaps down with a noise "of many waters." Opposite me is a mountain [the Ortstock] with huge rock walls and seven peaks rising one above the other. . . .
>
> O my Lord! What do you want to say to me today? Help me to hear your voice. Teach me to understand the language spoken by your creation all around me. Help me to receive into my innermost soul the great truth that, "To whom much is given, of them shall much be required." (LL)

The thought came to Hannah: *Why not write of the steps of my journey thus far, through difficulties and loneliness, battling pride and impatience?* These qualities had begun to seem to her to be tangible "enemies" who had tried to trip her up more than once. These thoughts were to wind their way through her imagination along with her ideas about the Christian life. Added to this was the influence of the classical literature she had read in her childhood; and it all combined to enable her to produce something entirely new and life-changing.

The Song of the Shepherd—that was it, the sweet music

that had kept her on the Way: through her days of Bible school, through journeys in Ireland and England with the Band, and throughout her God-blessed work in Israel, to that moment. Threads of a story were steadily coming together in her heart and mind—a way to share with people she would encounter *everywhere* the depth of God's working in the human soul. Gradually, the desire and inspiration to produce her allegory of the Christian life, *Hinds' Feet on High Places*, was beginning to form in her.

The lessons of Love were continually teaching and guiding her and giving her the insights that soon would bring her to put pen to paper in the most significant literary work of her life. But, as always, there were also practical considerations and everyday decisions that had to be made.

Where would she now live? Through what means would she be called to continue to bring the gospel to those close to her—and around the world? How much a part of this was writing books to be?

Returning to the state of Israel, she rejoined her colleagues. Through all their ongoing visiting work, the group continued to discover how Love himself was planning and going before them wherever they sought to bring his message, as wayfarers in the land. This at least was sure: They were to "walk in the Way," as they had been led, until further orders came.

One of these partners, Ruth Laurence, remembers how she and Hannah worked together in Israel, both in the early days of visiting every Jewish settlement and Arabic village and then in the unsettling days following statehood. For a time Ruth was living in the south and usually meeting once a month with Hannah and their other prayer partners. Excerpts from her diary provide an intimate look at Hannah's vision and continued labor in spite of the constantly changing conditions of the early 1950s:

1950. HRH [Hannah] expects to be at work this autumn in Northern Israel. She suggests fortnightly cooperation in the Haifa district. I should dearly love to be more closely with her in the work once more.

1951. A room is practically unobtainable still. A possible alternative is a good caravan [motorized van]. HRH has felt led to pray for one and is now rejoicing in a most wonderful offer of one, as well as marvelous help over other difficulties of buying and taking one to Israel, together with a new car for her work.

1952. Now the caravan has arrived in Israel at last . . . loaned until she returns from her extended tour "down under" [Australia, where Hannah was traveling to speak of her work in Israel]. . . . While over here another special joy was to see HRH again. She expects to be out in Israel next spring before continuing her South American tour.

These clues to Hannah's life after Israel's statehood—a time not otherwise well documented—begin to paint a clearer picture of the changing ministry that was unfolding for her. She was then in her forties, looking back at many years of intense visiting and speaking in Israel. Now she felt that God was calling her to an extension of the gospel ministry in which she had been engaged for the past twenty-six years. This would involve not only traveling and speaking around Israel and in her native Britain, but also being open to other worldwide opportunities: in Canada, New Zealand, and the United States. At about this time, too, she learned that a new Israeli edict prevented her from living in Israel permanently. Instead, she would make her home back in England and establish a base for international outreach there. One door was closed, but to her delight, others were opening.

Hannah kept busy writing more of her thoughts, especially in journal form, and was beginning to see this writing as a key part of her ministry. Additionally, many opportunities arose for her to speak to people interested in the evangelization that continued in Israel. These encouraging signs were combining with a growing support of committed intercessors—a prayer chain that eventually reached around the globe. With all of this, Hannah was heartened that her Lord was still directing her, even though her plans were of necessity being altered.

Along with traveling, Hannah soon acknowledged to herself that writing was to be a major part of her new ministry. In order to write, though, she needed to have times alone with her Lord, waiting on his voice and listening for direction as to what was to be recorded next—and how to write it. Finding the "trysting place" sometimes meant flying to another location where interruptions were few, where solitude and contemplation were possible, and where the beauty of nature could provide the peace she sought. Switzerland was just such a place for Hannah

And so it is fitting that it was on a vacation with Marjorie, her stepmother, to Braunwald, Switzerland, in 1955, that Hannah began her most famous work. The two women had gone to the mountains for rest and solitude. At the time, even Marjorie did not know that Hannah was busy compos-ing—while sitting on the green slopes overlooking the Or-tstock mountain—her story of Much-Afraid's journey with her Shepherd.

Hannah had written, during her visit to the Alps six years earlier, that she felt the Lord was speaking to *her* as he had to the Hebrew prophet Moses, "Come up to me into the mount . . ." (Exod. 24:12). Yet, just as that godly man was unable to see Yahweh face-to-face on Mt. Sinai, Hannah, too, had found that the mountain was covered in mist. But her faith was sure: "I believe that he will speak to me out of the cloud" (LL).

An allegory is, in a sense, a message out of a "cloud," or a story in which spiritual truths are revealed through the unraveling of fictional details. It is a narrative with charac-ters usually having the names of qualities such as Hope, Faith, and Sorrow. The most famous allegory in the English language, *Pilgrim's Progress*, with which Hannah was familiar, is such a narrative. Written by seventeenth-century English preacher John Bunyan, it stands high in the annals of spiri-tual literature of all time for its influence on generations of readers. Composed in the form of a dream, it follows the stages of the soul in its journey toward salvation. Bunyan's work has, through the years, been translated into several hundred languages worldwide and remains a classic of the Christian faith.

Hannah, with her education, sharp intellectual skills, and a heart to know God, was uniquely suited to write her own story of the soul's journey. Her choice of such a traditional form as allegory in which to write is a reflection of the sophistication and depth of her understanding and of her confidence in the gifts God had given her. *Hinds' Feet* is also filled with evidence of her love of nature. It reveals her discernment of God's process of teaching the soul to live in love with himself and others through the actual steps of one's life. At this point in her own life, Hannah could share many such stories. There were lessons from her times in Switzerland, of waterfalls and wildflowers, peaks and lowlands, relating to the heights and the valleys of human experience.

She was blessed with an abundance of knowledge of scriptural truth. And she had known much struggle, as well as triumph over difficulties, throughout her eventful life. So it was natural that, at this stage of her ministry, she would begin to record some of the lessons she had learned. With God's leading and blessing, their telling was to take shape in a most readable and edifying story. The experience of writing this work not only strengthened her own belief, but allowed her to share generously with literally millions of other people the source of her faith.

The steep slopes of Switzerland were, in one sense, the "High Places" to which Hannah's imagination naturally turned in the writing of *Hinds' Feet*. Yet, as she relates in her "Foreword to the Allegory" in the Olive Press edition of the book (1955), the inspiration for the setting came also from her experiences in Israel. And it grew out of her love for the Old Testament wisdom book, the Song of Solomon, also known as the Song of Songs or Canticles (abbreviated as "Cant." in her book).

An insight from one of her fellow workers also contributed to Hannah's setting of her allegory in a pastoral context. She related this incident in the foreword:

145

One morning during the Daily Bible Reading on our Mission Compound in Palestine, our little Arab nurse read from *Daily Light* a quotation from the Song of Songs. "The voice of my beloved! Behold, he cometh leaping upon the mountains, skipping upon the hills" (Song of Sol. 2:8). When asked what the verse meant, she looked up with a happy smile of understanding and said, "It means there are no obstacles which our Saviour's love cannot overcome, and that to Him, mountains of difficulty are as easy as an asphalt road!"

And of course Hannah remembered her years among the hills of Israel, which were reminiscent of the terrain common to the Psalms and the Song of Solomon. As she was also to write in the foreword to the first edition of *Hinds' Feet*:

"From the garden at the back of the Mission house at the foot of Mount Gerizim we could often watch the gazelles bounding up on the mountain-side, leaping from rock to rock with extraordinary grace and agility. Their motion was one of the most beautiful examples of exultant and apparently effortless ease in surmounting obstacles which I have ever seen."

All of these thoughts together were working steadily on Hannah's imagination as she began to *act* on her desire to write of the "High Places"—the destiny of those who seek Love himself.

Hinds' Feet on High Places begins in the Valley of Humiliation, where the young, crippled heroine, Much-Afraid, lives with her relatives, the Fearings, in a small white cottage in the village of Much-Trembling. This truly was Hannah herself before her conversion—before her liberation from her own handicaps, and especially from fear.

Much-Afraid is in the employ of the Chief Shepherd, whose flocks graze in these parts. Her greatest desire is to be made like the Shepherd himself—to overcome the handicap of her crippled legs and her crooked mouth with its broken speech. Through difficulty and misunderstanding, Much-Afraid finally escapes to go with the Shepherd. But to her dismay, he leaps on ahead, leaving two companions to guide her on the lower slopes—Sorrow and Suffering. There are hints that their true names will be revealed to her as she goes willingly with them.

It is perhaps significant that the first temptation to forsake the way, once she has begun it, comes from a family member named Pride. He is a strong, handsome, and tenacious male "cousin" who takes advantage of the fact that the Shepherd is temporarily out of sight. Pride appeals to her through flattery, though he had never paid any attention to her before she started to ascend.

How like life this is: When we are attempting to do the right thing, and know it, we are most vulnerable to pride. As conscientious and aware as she was, Hannah acknowledged that pride continued to be a temptation to her throughout her life. "It is a terrible thing to let Pride take one by the hand, Much-Afraid suddenly discovered. . . ."

But with one call to the Shepherd, Pride is deterred—though for a while after that, Much-Afraid finds herself limping more painfully than before.

At many points on the way, the heroine stops to build altars to the Lord, gathering "memorial stones" that she carries in a leather pouch. Meanwhile, her Fearing relatives, including Resentment, Bitterness, and Self-Pity, are searching for her in order to hinder her progress.

Finally, when the little company reaches the top of the highest hill, the mountains themselves come into sight. Though the way looks impassable, the hart and the hind, those natural inhabitants of the mountains, show them how to leap. This is the Mount of Injury, the place the Shepherd has chosen for Much-Afraid's particular ascent.

Throughout the journey, Much-Afraid is cheered by the songs from the Shepherd's old book, including these lines:

> Come with Me to the heights above,
> Yet fairer visions see
> . . . To where the dawn's clear innocence
> Bids all the shadows flee . . .

> The lions have their dens up there—
> The leopards prowl the glens up there
> But from the top the view is clear
> Of land yet to be won.

At this point the Shepherd again appears and informs her that she must next go through the Forests of Danger and Tribulation.

Through all of these experiences, Much-Afraid still remains true to her name. She is terrified at the prospect of traveling through the forests on the way to the High Places and fears that she will never have hinds' feet or reach her destination. Self-Pity and Resentment try to persuade her to try another, easier path. But Sorrow and Suffering intervene, and the three press on.

The heroine gradually learns to feel joy and pleasure in the company of her two helpers. As the travelers continue, they encounter obstacles such as the Valley of Loss, the Falls of Love, the Spring of Marah, or bitterness, and finally a chasm that stops them dead. Here the Shepherd meets them and tells Much-Afraid that this is the place where she is to make her offering. After an experience of death and resurrection, she is led to a miraculous healing stream of water, and when she steps into it, she is delivered from her crooked feet and mouth.

At this point, the call to ascend yet further to the High Places is overwhelming. She sees the hart and the hind spring up from the rock altar. With her new feet, she follows them to the precipice where the Shepherd meets her.

"Never am I to call you Much-Afraid again," he tells her. "I will write upon her a new name, the name of her God. 'The Lord God is a sun and shield: the Lord will give grace and glory: no good thing will he withhold from them that walk uprightly' (Ps. 84:11). This is your new name," he declares. "From henceforth you are Grace and Glory."

Next, he asks for the memorial stones, or promises, she has gathered, each representing the overcoming of a temptation to doubt. These are transformed into glorious, sparkling jewels, which he sets in a golden circlet for her to wear. Then two shining figures appear—Sorrow and Suffering, whose names are now revealed to be Joy and Peace, her companions all along.

Though she has arrived in the region of the High Places, Grace and Glory discovers that there is much more to ascend to, to see and understand on further journeys with her Shepherd. These are "beginners' slopes," and some heights remain accessible only to those who have finished their journey on

149

earth. Yet, from this vantage point, she can see all that she has been through in a different perspective. "She began to understand quite clearly that Truth cannot be understood from books alone or by any written words, but only by personal growth and development in understanding."

Hinds' Feet on High Places is a marvelous introduction to the Shepherd's Song as it is meant to be sung through each of our lives. It shows how God will work with a willing soul to teach the ways of the kingdom while we are still on earth. But we must ourselves take the journey in order truly to grasp the insights our Shepherd would teach us.

Hannah gave great credit to her stepmother, Marjorie, for the inspiration and encouragement to write the allegory. Marjorie recalls that when her stepdaughter finished writing *Hinds' Feet*, she took it first of all to her to read. Mrs. Hurnard was, at the time, running The Hill House Guest House in Colchester, England, for Christian workers and returning missionaries. She remembers that, upon reading the lovely story, she was enthralled and encouraged Hannah to publish it. Years later Hannah said to Marjorie, "I owe that book to you."

The first edition of *Hinds' Feet* was published in 1955 by Olive Press of CMJ, the missionary headquarters for the work in the Middle East that Hannah was involved in. In 1975 Tyndale House published the North American edition of the book, which remains in print in a number of translations and editions.

Hannah's hope for this most famous and dearly loved of her books was that it would facilitate a ministry of compassion. She wrote in the foreword to the first edition,

Perhaps the Lord will use it to speak comfort to some of

His loved ones who are finding themselves forced to keep company with Sorrow and Suffering, or who "walk in darkness and have no light," or feel themselves "tossed with tempest and not comforted." It may help them understand . . . the wonderful process by which the Lord is making real in their lives the same experience which made David and Habakkuk cry out exultantly, "The Lord God maketh my feet like hinds' feet, and setteth me upon mine High Places." (Ps. 18:33 and Hab. 3:19)

Hannah maintained an active correspondence through the years with many readers of her books. She said, "The letters that do come to me from various places, especially in the U.S.A., are from people who write to tell me how God has used the messages to help them in what seemed to be very great and distressing needs. I hear from people suffering from nervous breakdowns, from would-be suicides, lonely, terrified and often despairing who have been given the books. . . . I am grateful that they are available to such a multitude of people."

Avid readers of Hannah's books are abundant in number, fervent, and grateful for the beautiful, intimate portrait they paint of the spiritual life. A 1992 prayer letter from Dolores Wirz, a missionary with LIFE Ministries in Japan, contains this positive report:

One of the loveliest homemakers who has been attending my Friday morning English Bible class since its beginning in this area five years ago, at last decided to "confess with her mouth" the faith that has grown in her heart over the years. She identified with the character, "Much-Afraid," whose name was changed to "Grace & Glory" in the classic, *Hinds' Feet on High Places* by Hannah Hurnard. Pray that [she] will continue to grow in grace and glory as she pursues her journey of faith and tries to bring the good news of Jesus to her family and to fellow homemakers in the class.

The effect of *Hinds' Feet* on so many readers stands as the strongest testimony to its importance in the literature of Christianity. For example, the following letters represent some of the many praises of the work that have been received by Tyndale House Publishers since the publication of the American edition in 1977:

> *Hinds' Feet on High Places* was *wonderful*, best I have read in quite a while! The Lord has truly anointed Hannah as she writes of her life and her experiences. I feel as if I had known her all of my life. The things she describes are so intense, so soul-searching. I felt as though someone had looked into *my* soul, my innermost thoughts and then wrote them down on paper. I feel that through the circumstances of my everyday life, I was led down a path to eventually read this book. It has opened new doors in my life and given me an awareness of what life itself is meant to be. I definitely feel that through the words of Hannah's book I have been drawn much closer to the Lord than I would have been without reading it.
>
> —Betty, Kentucky, 1989

> I first read *Hinds' Feet* in 1975. . . . In October I picked it up again and by January had read it through five

times. Through it I was given the courage to go on. I was given a reason for suffering. I was able to let go of stiff resistance and to begin to melt into God's ways. God blessed. Since then I have read the series of eight [of Hannah's books] and have learned much.

—Judith Ann, Texas, 1989

Thank you for writing such a beautiful, powerful, glorious book [Hinds' Feet]. Wow! It took my breath away and made the tears flow. What an answer to how I should "accept"—"bear" and "obey." Many thanks.

—Joanne, British Columbia, 1988

I was so happy to be able to find other books by the author of Hinds' Feet on High Places that I bought all of them for my fifteen-year-old granddaughter! I gave her Hinds' Feet . . . when she was ten and she knows it almost by heart. She keeps rereading it! . . . Hannah Hurnard's books are . . . deep and inspiring, but the wonderfully graced gift of presentation should reach all if they reach a ten-year-old! [She has a] rare gift of lucidity in the spiritual realm.

—Katherine, Massachusetts, 1983

Through the years, Hinds' Feet has gained an increasingly wider audience through word of mouth and such deeply expressed appreciation. For readers drawn to a gentle, personal, and often poetic rendering of some of the deeper Christian truths, it has become a beloved introduction to the spiritual life.

The book has frequently been on Christian best-seller lists and was included among the "Premier 100" best-selling backlist books in *Bookstore Journal's* March 1993 report. Well over a million copies of this edition alone are in circulation.

Following the initial publication of *Hinds' Feet*, Hannah's list of published books began to grow, including further reflections based on her many years of ministry. Many of the books and booklets were first published by Olive Press for distribution by CMJ. One of the earliest works was her prayer diary of her missionary experiences in Israel, *Watchmen on the Walls*, which is no longer in print. Her other books published by Tyndale House include *Mountains of Spices*, *Hearing Heart* (an autobiography), *Wayfarer in the Land*, *God's Transmitters*, *Walking Among the Unseen*, *Kingdom of Love*, and *Winged Life*.

Mountains of Spices, a sequel to *Hinds' Feet*, tells further of the life of Grace and Glory. It describes the ninefold fruit of the Spirit from Galatians 5:22-23, which is shown to correspond to the nine spices in the "garden enclosed" and the "orchard of pomegranates" in Song of Solomon 4:13-14. In this book, Hannah's poetic gifts shine and spiritual insights abound, as they do in *Hinds' Feet*.

However, in the third book of the series, *Eagles' Wings to the Higher Places*, many readers find quite a departure from the earlier two allegories. *Eagles' Wings* follows the story of Aletheia, the daughter of Grace and Glory and her husband, Fearless Witness. Aletheia (Love of Truth) has lived all her life on the High Places and is called to the valleys below to persuade others to climb to the Kingdom of Light and Love.

What actually occurs in this book seems less a "Shepherd's Song" than a plea of Hannah's own that readers be brought to the "higher truth" to which she herself turned in her later years. The view that she strongly sets forth is one of universalism, or a belief that *all will be saved in the end*. This was an understanding that caused Hannah to reconsider all of her early evangelical zeal, as well as to look with new eyes at the meaning of life and death. She shows, through fictional narrative, how she entered a new stage of belief that is troublesome to many readers of her later books, especially those holding to an orthodox Christian faith.

How did this change come about, and what are its implications for the legacy of Hannah Hurnard, her work, and her life?

Eleven

THE WAY
IS NOT EASY

*Let us run with patience the particular race
that God has set before us.*

Hebrews 12:1, TLB

*Sometimes, as she looked on the glorious pan-
orama visible from these lowest slopes in the
Kingdom of Love, she found herself blushing
as she remembered some of the dogmatic statements which she and others had made in the
depths of the valley about the High Places and
the ranges of Truth. They had been able to see
so little and were so unconscious of what lay
beyond and above. . . . Even up on those wonderful slopes she was only looking out on a tiny
corner of the whole.*

from Hinds' Feet on High Places

L ike many other middle-aged people, I was growing very
dissatisfied with myself and my life," Hannah wrote in
Walking Among the Unseen. "I meant so well and longed to
be of use, but somehow I seemed to be so dreadfully powerless, so unable to help people in their sorrows, sufferings, and
sicknesses as I longed to do, and as I believe we are all meant
to be able to do.

"I talked about this lack of power to the Lord, and he said,
'First of all, child, you must understand that in the Kingdom
of heaven no one majors on the faults and failures of other
people, or the irritating wrong things that they do. . . . Don't
feed yourself a constant diet of thoughts about the things

that you don't like or don't agree with, or of which you disapprove, or which cause you to feel irritation, anger, resentfulness, jealousy, or any other unlovely feelings.'"

This was another stage of transformation that Hannah credits to a shift in her perspective. She acknowledged that the biggest changes in her life and her viewpoints came in the 1950s. That mixed experience, like life itself, contained both negative and positive aspects.

To her great joy, she received even further physical healing. All of her symptoms of stammering vanished. Her lifelong condition of anemia eased. There was deliverance from exhaustion and debilitating fatigue. Finally, she felt relief from the neuralgia pains in her head, plus rheumatic back and shoulder aches that had plagued her through the last rigorous years of her work in Israel.

When she wrote in *Mountains of Spices* of Grace and Glory's return to the valley to try to help her relatives find the Shepherd, Hannah knew from experience exactly what some of the heroine's problems would be and how to communicate them. The characters Pride and Superiority embodied traits she understood well because they stood for her own weaknesses. Irritation with others with whom she did not agree was a recurrence of the old battle she herself had always had with egotism and her own "specialness." In the past, such pride had caused Hannah to have difficulties in her work with people.

In her nonfiction books on spirituality, such as *Walking Among the Unseen*, Hannah courageously wrote of these inner conflicts with which she continued to wrestle—when she could have kept up a front and rested on the laurels of her ever-more-successful speaking and writing career.

Further, Hannah began increasingly to open herself to some new approaches to "inner healing" and to practice what she called "holy harmlessness." This was the idea that "the harmless cannot be harmed." In this "new" approach to life, she felt she was being especially directed by Christ to think only pure, loving thoughts, and to maintain a positive attitude toward all people and events—certainly an admirable goal. Yet along with these idealistic views, she had some blind spots about important practical matters, such as her own personal health, which were quite troublesome.

By 1952 Hannah was spending part of her time in Israel and the rest of the year in her native Essex, ministering to people from both places, as well as throughout her travels. Supremely self-sufficient, she lived alternately in a little house just outside Tiberias and in a cottage on Mersea Island, Essex, which she used to visit as a child. While on the island, she loved to talk to the young children staying in trailers for their summer holidays. They, in turn, took great delight in the lovely stories and poems this vibrant Christian lady shared. Hannah tried to take advantage of every opportunity that presented itself to encourage and enlighten listeners by sharing her own faith and beliefs.

However, her friends and family were finding it increasingly difficult to travel with Hannah down the road she was choosing. Moving gradually toward unorthodox views, she was to find that by openly expressing her individualistic ideas about diet and spirituality, she would alienate more and more people. When she voiced other, even more questionable viewpoints in her public speaking engagements, door after door would close to her. Eventually, all invitations to speak to evangelical Christian groups virtually came to an end.

Nevertheless, she continued to write and speak to those who were open to her message, seeking diligently to convert others to her new ways of thinking.

Yet some people were attracted to her approach. For fifteen years, from 1967 to 1982, she wrote, printed, and distributed from her home in England free booklets twice a year to a growing mailing list of supporters around the world. In 1982 printing costs in Britain increased so as to make continued free circulation of the booklets and an accompanying newsletter impossible. So Hannah turned over the distribution of the remaining copies to a colleague in the United States.

Throughout the years following her work in Israel, Hannah led an active life of furthering her message among groups such as Camps Farthest Out. Under the direction of Dr. Glenn Clark, this organization shared Hannah's belief that greater planes of spiritual understanding could and must be reached by individuals who felt so called—even if it meant going "beyond" the camp of traditional orthodoxy.

In her third allegory, *Eagles' Wings to the Higher Places*, she includes a chapter on being "Outside the Camp," as well as a poem she wrote to that effect. In that work of fiction, she speaks of the "horrified reactions" of the heroine's friends to her new views, which caused "utmost distress . . . from many quarters" and "the strongest possible condemnation." Nothing could better describe what actually happened in the context of Hannah's own ministry at this point, and what it cost her in terms of her readership and the ears of a wider audience.

During the 1980s Hannah wrote of her changed perspectives in several books: *Eagles' Wings to the Higher Places*

(1983), *Steps to the Kingdom* (1985), *Way of Healing* (1986), and *Thou Shalt Remember* (1988), all published by Harper & Row. A recent posthumously published book of Hannah's writings, *The Inner Man* (Sun Publishing, 1993), clearly reflects what has come to be known as "New Age" thinking.

Hannah's autobiographical book, *Thou Shalt Remember*, gives perhaps the clearest description of her altered emphases. In this book she recounts her "conversion" to a more universalistic view of God's love for all creatures (including all of nature, and especially animals, which she began to refuse as food). She talked about a "spiritual body" that could transcend normal physical barriers to comfort others. A desire of hers was to return to a "Garden of Eden" approach to the physical world, in which no flesh is ever eaten and all forms of life are respected as having "rights" and, therefore, are to be treated with love.

One of the most telling examples of Hannah's changed thinking about salvation and its scope can be found by comparing her telling of an incident in *Wayfarer in the Land* and her later retelling and reflection on it in *Thou Shalt Remember*.

In the earlier book she relates an event that occurred when she was working among Moslem people in the Jordan Valley in the early 1930s. Because terrorist gangs were a continual threat to travelers then, a curfew existed on roads all over the country. One night, just at sunset, Hannah was asked if she was willing to drive a woman to a hospital about twenty miles away in Nazareth. The Moslem woman had just given birth and was in serious condition. Hannah readily agreed and ended up taking her, the midwife, and the husband, as well as the two-hour-old baby. It was surely the most harrowing ride Hannah had ever taken, even in *that* country. She wrote:

> It was quite dark, and as there was curfew the track [there was no real road] was of course completely deserted. It was terribly rough and bumpy . . . the strangest ride of my life. Just as we came to the foot of these hills, the full moon rose over Mount Tabor on our right, flooding the whole landscape with silvery light.
>
> Suddenly the young woman I was transporting in the back of the car became unconscious. Then the husband lost all control of himself and fell shrieking on top of his wife.
>
> The midwife thrust the swaddled baby she had been holding into my arms. While she was trying to tear the husband off the young mother, I, with the baby in one arm, was searching frantically for a piece of iron we could force between the clenched teeth of the dying woman. Then I laid the baby on the empty seat beside me and, supporting her with one hand, began the ascent of the hairpin bends up the mountain. . . .
>
> At that moment I was so vividly conscious of the presence of the Lord Jesus himself, that it seemed he was almost visible. Up and up the car twisted. . . . The whole scene is fixed in my memory like an over-exposed photograph, in sharp blacks and whites. . . .
>
> At last we came to the town on the mountaintop, and drove up to the door of the hospital. . . . In a moment or two the doctor and his stretcher bearers came and lifted out the unconscious woman. She was laid on the operating table and died that very moment.

The long agonizing ride had been in vain. This woman had died without hearing of Christ the Savior.

Hannah was still clutching the newborn baby in her arms, and the woman's husband was sobbing in despair beside her. "At that moment I turned in silence to the Lord, with an almost desperate questioning of the heart," she recalled.

"Why did you let us make such an effort to save this woman's body, and yet give her no opportunity to hear the message of life? Where has she gone now? Is there any use at all in all our mission work? She is just one among a *multitude* of other souls leaving this world in ignorance and darkness. Only she died among Christians, and yet never had an opportunity to hear of Christ." . . .

This experience made a lasting impression on me. It was not that I felt afterwards that it did not matter so much if we did not urgently seek the lost before they left this world, for in the end all will be well. Rather, it was an overwhelming sense of our Lord's passionate love and longing for the souls of all whom he has created, and his determination to seek them at all costs, and his longing that *we should cooperate with him in this work* (italics added).

Hannah's explanation here is in agreement with her message in *Mountains of Spices*. In that allegory she emphasizes, *not* a universal salvation, but the fact that Jesus Christ has suffered once for the sin of all mankind and longs and travails for everyone to come to him for salvation. Expressed in her own words:

All pangs of sin's disease so dread
Are suffered by Our Thorn-crowned Head. . . .

So One with us He will not part
E'en from the hardest self-willed heart . . .
In Christ shall all men live again. . . .

Interestingly, in this book, the character Lord Fearing does
die without turning in repentance to the Shepherd (Christ).
"Death" comes to him, "touching him with ice-breath" to
whisper: "Thou fool! this night is thy soul required of thee."
This scene is clearly to serve as a reminder that one must not
put off accepting salvation, or death can rob one of the
choice. In that it is reminiscent of the New Testament warning that "now is the day of salvation" (2 Cor. 6:2). G. K.
Chesterton once pointed out that Jesus never said that a man
would lose his soul, but that he must *take care* that he did not
lose his soul. While we are in time, we must choose.

Therefore, the thrust of *Mountains of Spices* is overwhelmingly on the side of *transformation of souls who do find life
through the Shepherd*. Many more doubters and fearers, such
as Much-Afraid once was, turn to climb to the High Places
and there receive new names befitting their redeemed life.
Even the terrible suitor Craven Fear is broken and renewed
to become Fearless Witness—and the husband of Grace and
Glory.

Hannah did a great deal of thinking about the death of the
Moslem woman over the years. Remembrance of her reaction to it seems crucial in her shift in belief to a form of
universalism—a conviction that every soul will be saved in
the end, since Christ is the Savior of all. Her meditation on
this subject in *Thou Shalt Remember* takes on a mystical cast

when she has the Lord speaking to her of this remembered event:

> "Hannah, don't you think that when that Moslem woman breathed her last breath on the hospital stretcher and her earthly consciousness ended, that the first thing she would become aware of would be me telling her that I loved her and was there with her, ready to take her home to our Father and to his eternal love? There she would be able to hear everything about me that she never had the opportunity to hear on earth and respond with all her own heart's love." . . .
>
> From that night on I have never doubted the glorious fact that he is indeed "the Savior of all men" *and women.* Not a single soul is lost forever! The loving Savior gets a one hundred percent victory and the devil gets none [so that we are] able to love and adore and worship him to a far greater degree than would ever have been possible if we had not fallen into sin and experienced his forgiving love. For as the Savior himself said, "He that is forgiven much, loveth much." (pp. 92–93)

Hannah's theological explanation of this shift in viewpoint is a mystical one: "For every single soul is to be rescued and saved; indeed each one is undergoing that blessed process now and finally will be able to cooperate with our triumphant Father God in creating nothing but the highest possible good" (TSR).

Hannah was to receive many reactions to the viewpoints expressed in her later writings about such issues as after-death experiences. To her puzzlement, she was told that her

perspective had become "metaphysical." She wrote in a letter to the editor-in-chief of Tyndale House in 1976:

> I must say this surprised me very much and I had to turn
> to the dictionary to find the meaning. . . .
>
> I do seem to meet a number of metaphysically inter-
> ested people, and Spiritualists and many unorthodox
> people who do not go to religious services, indeed all
> the people who would never come to listen to me when
> I was sharing the good news in the churches. My heart
> goes out to them, for they seem to be in such desperate
> need, under stresses of all kinds, frantically seeking for,
> and not finding, real Highest delivering truth, which
> was brought by our Saviour Jesus.
>
> I always tell them that there is a much, much better
> and safer way than spiritualistic, psychic and occult
> methods. We do not need to contact discarnate spirits
> on very low levels of spiritual understanding, but we can
> meet our Lord and all the living members in His Body
> "in the heavenly places" in His beautiful presence.

Thus she continued to use rather ambiguous language to
bridge the growing gap between her former orthodox writings and the newer mystical or metaphysical statements she
was making in her personally distributed pamphlets and in
her newer books.

For instance, she needed to explain how the process of
continual striving to reach this higher plane of spiritual
communion would operate. To satisfy this, Hannah came to
believe that in order to have a chance to grow into the full
truth of God and God's ways, one would have to be allowed
more than one lifetime. Yet she asserted that *when,* in one

allotted lifetime, *a soul was somehow able to become purged* of such "longing" and to learn the "glorious message that earth life is meant to teach us," that soul would not need to return to another lifetime on earth, but would *then* receive "eternal life."

In *Thou Shalt Remember,* Hannah's writing is somewhat ambiguous as to how this relates to Eastern religions that teach the doctrine of reincarnation. On the other hand, she is clear in her declaration that it is always *turning to Jesus* that leads to a life in which we "die no more." Somehow, through considering her experience of the death of the Moslem woman, pondering her reactions at the time, and adding the insights that came to her later, she arrived at her particular views.

Many readers greatly appreciate and seek to live by Hannah's earlier books but react with confusion and disappointment at her shift in viewpoint. In a statement in *Bookstore Journal* in May 1990, Tyndale House vice president Wendell Hawley said: "Tyndale House remains pleased to be the publisher of Hannah Hurnard's earlier books—written while she was a missionary in Israel under Church's Ministry Among the Jews. Miss Hurnard is a very capable Bible student and demonstrates a deep love for the Lord Jesus; however, in her later books she espouses several ideas with which we do not agree, nor wish to propagate."

Hannah's response at that time was:

> The messages in the later books point to the Lord Jesus as the way to real God-consciousness and union with His will—not just by believing doctrines about Him, but by studying and practicing the blessed precepts [he]

taught. . . . These later books *are read mostly by people who find themselves unable to believe the religious teachings that they were taught.*

Because they were not helped by them to make real contact with God's presence and delivering and saving power, they attend no place of worship. . . . I owe an eternal debt of gratitude to my evangelical parents and the Keswick Convention in England in 1924 for starting me on the journey to real contact with God and life in Him. But every year that passes, He is lovingly teaching me to understand more about His divine grace, love, and power and determination to rescue and restore everyone from their fallen, lost condition.

In fact, in the later years of her life, Hannah herself ceased to attend any church. Her lifelong conviction that God would speak to her personally, giving her deeper and deeper insights and "light" that was to be widely shared with others, led her to believe that there could be no spiritual authority over her or her speaking and writing except the Lord Jesus himself.

Hannah continued to receive critical letters from evangelical readers concerning her change in beliefs. But she made it clear that she allowed herself to think no "negative" thoughts or to allow such criticism to move or change her in any way. She would entertain no visitors unless they agreed to be taught by her—rather than to challenge or question her beliefs.

For the remainder of her life, Hannah continued earnestly to believe in the importance of perpetuating this "new light," found on the "even Higher Places," including the necessity of certain holy harmless practices such as not eating meat. She would share these strongly held convictions and seek to persuade others of this "way," both publicly and privately, whenever she was given the opportunity.

Once in the early 1980s when she visited one of her publishing houses, Hannah shared that she was a fruitarian. She brought her own lunch in a plain brown paper sack. In it were several "fruits," including a tomato, which were chosen by a strict definition as allowable in her diet. Declining an invitation to dine out at one of the local restaurants, she consented to picnicking outdoors instead.

In 1984, at age seventy-nine, Hannah finally had to give up her home in Israel. She called her stepmother to say that she was very ill, asking if she could stay with her for two weeks to recover. Marjorie's pastor in England, the Reverend Maurice Richards, drove up to the airport to meet Hannah. Due to her weakened condition, she arrived in a wheelchair. According to the pastor, she looked as though she were about to die.

Marjorie had thoughtfully arranged for a Red Cross nurse to go with Pastor Richards to the airport and had sent them in her own Wolseley car. The medical assistance proved invaluable. Once back in Colchester, the nurse took Hannah upstairs and put her directly to bed, where she ended up staying for a recovery of not two weeks, but seven! Her body was full of acid because she had been eating only fruit. Rice and lentils were added to her diet, which helped her health improve steadily.

Hannah was not an easy patient to care for, Marjorie remembers. Despite these difficulties, and the fact that her stepdaughter's universalist views shocked her, the two women remained close throughout the remainder of Hannah's life.

Ursula Jones (widow of the late Reverend Hugh Jones of Christ Church, Jerusalem) was one of Hannah's friends and colleagues. She remembers that Hannah frequently suffered from vitamin deficiencies, as she did not eat properly. "She had some idea only to live on nuts and other tidbits" for survival, Mrs. Jones recalls. After Hannah moved to the United States, Mrs. Jones kept in touch with her, despite doubts about some of her theological opinions. Both she and her husband always remembered the help that Hannah had put forth tirelessly for the work during the war years (1948 on) in Jerusalem.

When Hannah had recuperated enough to be able to care for herself again, she was driven by friends to her own home on Mersea Island. She had written in Marjorie's visitors' book on August 31, 1984, of her "loving gratitude for forty-eight years of loving-kindness and friendship."

One cannot help but respect the single-mindedness, personal sacrifice, diligence, and sincerity of this great woman. Still, the question remains as to how much of her later personal beliefs are truly applicable or useful in the Christian life. Hannah's admirers seem to be divided into two groups: those who appreciate her life and works *before* she had these views and those who have turned to her after she embraced her new views.

What are we to make of such a change in a Christian leader's focus? What happened to this pillar of orthodoxy along the way, which led her to shift from emphasizing central Christian truths, to proclaiming, at best, marginal—at worst, heretical—views?

I, too, have struggled with these doubts and questions as I have read and studied her works. In the next chapter, we will attempt to see what is there and how we can view this shift in Hannah Hurnard's thinking, as fellow Christians, with charity and greater understanding.

Twelve

THE
HIGH
PLACES

Love accepts and loves all who truly love the Lord Jesus and make him central in their hearts. Then love bears all that irks and burdens and disappoints us in those we are put to work with and with whom we find we disagree. And love learns to pray for all such creatively, so that transforming power is liberated in their lives.

from Kingdom of Love

The kingdom of God is not eating and drinking, but righteousness and peace and joy in the Holy Spirit. . . . Therefore let us pursue the things which make for peace and the things by which one may edify another.

Romans 14:17, 19, NKJV

What can we learn from Hannah Hurnard's rich and complex legacy of writings over a long and eventful lifetime?

There are many spiritual lessons to be gleaned from Hannah's earlier books, especially as they illuminate certain phases of their author's life. At times, especially in *Hinds' Feet,* it is clear how the two realities—literary and actual life—interrelate in Hannah's recollection of events and their consequences. And yet, since a dramatic shift occurred in her focus through the years, readers need to evaluate carefully her various writings and beliefs. We would do well to consider the following guidelines as we do so.

First, as difficult as it is, we are not to judge her personally. In Romans 14 it is clear that, among Christians, "He who eats, eats to the Lord, for he gives God thanks; and he who does not eat, to the Lord he does not eat, and gives God thanks. . . . But why do you judge your brother?" (vv. 6, 10, NKJV). Scripture clearly allows for differing conscientious convictions about diet and other personal dedications that may not be "wrong" for one but can definitely be wrong for another if they come between that person and his or her worship of God. Such beliefs, in past ages of the church, were respected and referred to as "pious opinion." Hannah herself expressed this attitude well in the chapter "Unity of Love" in *Kingdom of Love* (reprinted in appendix 2 of this book). She wrote that Christians do not need to apply their faith in the same ways or patterns—or relentlessly to seek to persuade others to adopt what are, in essence, personal convictions.

We are all called individually to test and examine every idea in the light of Scripture, and "each of us shall give account of himself to God" (v. 12). And, as has always been the case, different Christians will come up with sometimes variant interpretations of some of the more ambiguous teachings of God's Word. Then there are the issues of whether they apply to an age gone by or still stand as commands or principles for us today, or both.

An example of this is Hannah's teaching that we ought to return to being "Eden people" by eating no meat. Is it truly possible, or even desirable, to return to such a level of consciousness as Adam and Eve held before sin entered the world?

According to early church history, the apostle Peter was

shown a vision by God about the eating habits of the Jews, "like a great sheet bound at the four corners, descending to him and let down to the earth. In it were all kinds of four-footed animals of the earth, wild beasts, creeping things, and birds of the air. And a voice came to him, 'Rise, Peter; kill and eat.' But Peter said, 'Not so, Lord! For I have never eaten anything common or unclean [by Jewish law].' And a voice spoke to him again the second time, 'What God has cleansed you must not call common'" (Acts 10:11-15, NKJV).

Jesus himself declared us free from laws that had "ruled" people for centuries. One such example is the Jewish purification rites, which his disciples were seen breaking by not washing their hands before eating (Matt. 15:2, 11). The Lord's reply to the critics was: "Not what goes into the mouth defiles a man; but what comes out of the mouth . . . evil thoughts, murders, adulteries, fornications, thefts, false witness, blasphemies. These are *the things* which defile a man, but to eat with unwashed hands does not defile a man" (Matt. 15:11, 19-20, NKJV). There was a foreshadowing of this truth in earlier Israelite history: "For the Lord does not see as man sees; for man looks at the outward appearance, but the LORD looks at the heart" (1 Sam. 16:7, NKJV).

Not all Christians choose to exercise all of the freedoms they are given, and often for good reason. In 1 Corinthians 8 the apostle Paul wrote about the qualms some Christians had about eating meat that had been offered in sacrifice to pagan gods and then sold in the marketplace. Although Paul knew such "gods" were not real and the meat was harmless, he urged some believers to abstain from eating it in order to avoid offending fellow Christians who had doubts about its propriety. "If meat make my brother to offend, I will eat no flesh while the world standeth," he boldly proclaimed (1 Cor. 8:13). Some people today choose not to eat meat for dietary reasons or because of cruelty in the handling of the animals raised to be slaughtered. All of these are legitimate issues to discuss, pray about, and act on as conscience dictates. But they should not be used as a sword to judge and alienate fellow Christians.

Second, besides reaching us through the beautiful language of the Holy Scriptures, God's truth has also been adapted and communicated by gifted and clearly God-directed writers, such as the earlier Hannah Hurnard. Readers are free to "live" within the context of a given story for its duration, to suffer with Much-Afraid as we see parallels of our own journey to the vocation and life of love to which our Shepherd leads us.

Its human author was a guide to us for a time. We may gratefully accept her insights and the sharing of her vision in *Hinds' Feet*, without needing to apologize or explain it in the context of what she might have done or not done later in her own life. A reader is not required to go "outside" a work, as some critics do, to debunk or reevaluate it in the light of an author's personal life events. That God spoke and worked through Hannah's inspirational allegories and many other of her numerous writings, and continues to do so, is undeniable. The evidence is in readers' testimonials and changed lives.

Third, none of us is big enough to contain or absorb all that God will teach humans. Each of us has only some of the truth, as Hannah herself wisely expressed in *Hinds' Feet*. Describing Grace and Glory's view from the Heights, she wrote: "Even up on those wonderful slopes she was only looking out on a tiny corner of the whole." She saw that from any vantage point, we see only a one-person view of the universe—even when we think we are in the place to which God has brought us. In God's mercy, it is all that we need to know at that point.

Fourth, we can read any of Hannah Hurnard's writings with which we do not agree to gain insight: a sharpening of our mind and a touching of our heart as to our own personal vulnerabilities. While we can only rejoice with Hannah in the vision of love for all creatures, which was granted to her in moments of insight in her earthly life, we cannot assume that these experiences should be developed into theories of universalism. When we start attempting to offer exact descriptions or explanations of *what God must do* to save sinners or *how everything is going to work out in the end*, we actually try to go farther than the Bible itself does. Even Jesus said that some things are known only to the Father—God alone (Matt. 24:36).

In his insightful work *The Great Divorce*, C. S. Lewis spoke wisely, warning that we "can know nothing of the end of all things, or nothing expressible in those terms. It may be, as [it has been said], that all will be well. . . . But it's ill talking of such questions. The question is asked, 'Because they are too terrible?' and the careful answer is given: 'No. Because all answers deceive.'" That is, he explains, because we necessarily look at such eternal questions through the lens of time. All we can see is what we need to know *for ourselves*, that being: "The choice of ways is before you. Neither is closed. Any man may choose eternal death. Those who choose it will have it . . . [but] every attempt to see the shape of eternity except through the lens of Time distorts your knowledge of freedom."*

We need not personally adopt or endorse any "explainable" scheme of how God's total plan of salvation will entirely work out. Indeed, Lewis cautions that we *must not*. In scriptural end-times admonitions, there are always two important elements. One is *our own responsibility for ethical living and proclaiming the Good News* until that end might come. The other is *symbolic representations of cataclysmic upheavals, which will alert us to the Messiah's return to our planet*. We would do well to read and hear the admonishing Word of God as it speaks to each of us.

Fifth, in order to be strengthened and supported to bear any truth at all, believers need each other. Besides the Holy Spirit, Christians need mature guides who will balance and enable them in their desire to understand and follow God's Word. We need to be accountable to the church, the body of believers, so as to *practice* our faith wisely. Such interdependence should steer each of us away from foolishness, imbalance, and going off on tangents; and it may bless us with the sweet fellowship of shared belief and the richness of living in kingdom ways.

We must learn to listen when others point out dangers in the way we are headed, particularly when two or more people whom we respect and trust—and who do not have a vested interest in our actions—warn us about our path. If we learn to listen, these wise others may draw us back to God's revealed words of Scripture, as well as to the tradition of

*C. S. Lewis, *The Great Divorce* (New York: Macmillan Publishing Co., 1946), 124–125.

belief, and to the worship in community that has brought us to that point.

Sixth, no written work, even if seemingly timeless, is equal to the Bible in the limitlessness of its wisdom and resources. For the Christian, any work should be read in conjunction with the Scriptures as the primary source of written truth. Authors, speakers, and other authorities—even if they are world-renowned and much-revered—are still fallible human beings. We must not expect any one individual, except the Lord, to give us wholly what we each personally need to help us live on the "High Places" God has called us to. But we are gratified to pick up bits and pieces of truth—to gather parables and principles and wise sayings—to aid us in the process of maturing our character and developing service for the kingdom. God's special written revelation constrains us, lest we burst into uncontrollable zeal without function or limits.

How God wants to use our effervescence in the kingdom! Hannah herself wrote, in *Hearing Heart*, "Bubbling, frothing new wine cannot continue to spill and splash over for ever. It must be constrained and confined in some way, or it will never become mellowed and sweetened and made ready for its best use." Indeed, in her earlier times of enthusiasm and reaction to other people's styles of worship, the young woman found herself needing to bite her critical tongue. She had to learn to let her own zeal and personal style be channeled into the peaceful presence of Love himself. Not until she ascertained Jesus' own patience and his purpose for her waiting could Hannah come to a place of using her remarkable creativity and effervescent gifts in a more positive way.

We, too, are born for and guided on an earthly pilgrimage

with a purpose: to prepare our minds and hearts for those same High Places that Hannah longed for during her life. Often it is the very differences among us that seem to thwart "our" purpose and against which we sometimes chafe, that may also enable our witness to become sharpened, "mellowed and sweetened and made ready for its best use," as she herself wrote.

Finally, we must always call upon the name of Jesus and seek to know him better in our daily walk. He is truly our best friend, our Shepherd who makes life full and complete and keeps us from harm until the time when we, like Hannah, are finally called into his presence.

CMJ director John Wood concludes that

> although Hannah's later writings differed from the works she published while she magnificently served in the ranks of CMJ . . . personally, I felt it right to maintain the very closest possible relationship with her, even though her theological views differed from mine at vital points. I continue to honor her and her work very highly indeed.
>
> To the end, Hannah was engaged in the cure of souls. People found it easy to open up to her. Her perception of people was incisive. Her words struck home. She was a godly counselor and a wise and warm woman.

Thirteen

A
FINAL
CALL

*Look! I have been standing at the door, and I
am constantly knocking. If anyone hears me
calling him and opens the door, I will come in
and fellowship with him and he with me.*

Revelation 3:20, TLB

*We can't unsee what we have seen,
    But ask God to show more,
And lead us on to richer truths
    Than we could see before.*

*His love will teach our still dimmed eyes,
    And we shall come to see
More of His wondrous love and grace
    Through all eternity.*

Hannah Hurnard, in a letter dated September 11, 1988

In 1984 Hannah left Colchester, England, to move to the United States. She spent her remaining years between the home of her friend and colleague Bernadette Fletcher in Lowell, Massachusetts, and her own home on Marco Island, Florida. In her modestly furnished, one-story town house off the southwestern coast of Florida, she was assisted by Mrs. Fletcher with her practical needs. Anyone who wished to see her for the purposes of hearing about "living on the Higher Places," learning about her writings, or receiving counsel and prayer was welcome to visit and talk with her. She also accepted and answered readers' letters and remained in contact with her publishers. Always, she exuded a positive and encouraging attitude. Her words of advice from a June 18, 1988, letter to John Wood were:

Be willing to obey God;
Trust He will guide aright,
Ask Him to block wrong pathways,
Wait till He gives more light.

The semitropical atmosphere of Marco Island lent itself to a slower, more leisurely lifestyle. Still, Hannah studied diligently and voraciously read the Bible and other books. Even with her failing health, she was known to carry her books around the house, sometimes as many as twenty filling her arms as she carted them from her bedroom to her study and back again.

She held an open house, which was not advertised, nearly every Monday night. People just came, and Hannah was generous with her time, as long as people would listen to her beliefs and respect her views and her guidance. The teaching sessions extended until about three weeks before her death.

As long as she was physically able, Hannah took long early morning and evening walks along the beach and could often be seen ambling along with a staff in her hand to keep her—strong as she was—from being thrown off balance when powerful, salty waves would reach her. She always seemed to be meditating during these walks and during the time she spent outdoors in her yard under a small pavilion, looking out on nature.

During these later years, Hannah suffered from colon cancer, which eventually hastened her death. Preferring homeopathic treatment, she refused to go to a traditional medical doctor or obtain conventional medication for several years. When, in 1989, she finally became hospitalized, she told the doctor that she was ready to die, wanted to do so, and that was why she had come. To the few who saw her, she appeared to be "in control" of her choices to the end. She was told that unless she desired life-sustaining treatment, which she decidedly did not, she should return home. That was her heart's desire.

Surprisingly, Hannah lived productively and cheerfully for eight more months. She denied having extensive suffering during this time, admitting only to some minor irritations or side effects. In the last week of her life, she was confined to her bed, and she died early on the morning of May 3, 1990. She had written one more poem just hours beforehand:

> Be on the watch all day to see
> The lovely things God does for me.
> And watch how blessings great evolve
> And every problem He will solve.
> The heavenly places are right here
> And I need nothing dread or fear.
> Oh, what a wondrous journey's end
> Safe in the arms of my best Friend.
> I, Hannah Hurnard, testify
> This is a lovely way to die.

EPILOGUE

We have explored, in this spiritual biography, what one faithful human being has demonstrated of the life of service.

Certainly, Hannah was one who allowed herself to be a channel of God's love. Sacrificially giving herself to active service, she used her mind, heart, and will to build up, to the best of her understanding, God's kingdom on the earth. Hers was a complete dedication as an evangelist and speaker to often hostile hearers and through constant perils and problems.

Yet, before her conversion to Christianity, Hannah had never been truly joyful. From that point on, though, this God-fearing woman took the high road, seeking ever greater heights of service, in spite of serious difficulties. After her extraordinary healing, a continuing speech impediment in daily conversation tended to keep her at arm's length from her peers; but she was able to preach unfalteringly to large gathered groups in England and Ireland, where her early missionary training took place.

Following such an uncharted course of itinerant evangelistic work was unprecedented for a woman in her day. Hannah overcame further obstacles—both physical and spiritual—in her challenging vocation. Laboring in the hot, exhausting climate of Palestine, she drove on dusty roads that were nothing but shifting sand and rocky mountain tracks in her miniature British Austin car, usually with only one female companion. This incredible woman braved unexpected rigors of ministry in Palestine during the early days of the modern Jewish-Arab turmoil.

Choosing to yield not to her former fears but rather to the power of Christ within her, she dared to give Hebrew New Testaments to Orthodox Jews, as well as witness boldly to Arabs and Moslems. She successfully shared her faith in God in Irish, English, and Middle Eastern villages and settlements even through times of civil and world wars.

Her *Hinds' Feet on High Places* remains an enduring inspirational classic. Since its publication, it has contributed a fullness of experience and meaning to the Christian journey to more than a million readers. As we have seen, it is the story of one soul, not unlike Hannah herself, guided by the loving Shepherd, who chose to take the difficult steps from the Valley of Humiliation up to the joy and wonder of the High Places. There, among the heights, she would—like Hannah—find the surefootedness of the hind and other mountain creatures.

Despite her desire to be a humble worker along with her colleagues, assertive Hannah always stood out. She remained personally independent even though she became part of a mission effort with clear purposes and guidelines. Her inner life of prayer and the certainty of God's leading her gave her this outwardly strong demeanor. Due to her family's wealth and support, she was able to make many of her own decisions about the course of her service.

The Hurnard family gave generously, through the years, to missionary efforts. The royalties from Hannah's classic spiritual works went to the Church's Ministry Among the Jews, rather than to her personal estate. (The exception to this was *Walking Among the Unseen*, whose sales helped support her in her final years.) It was clear that everything was on the altar for Hannah.

Like Moses, Hannah experienced God's call to the higher life of service. Surely, her childhood struggles were enough to make her identify with the Hebrew patriarch who also was, at first, resistant to being called by God. Though her name in Hebrew does mean "grace," there were physical barriers in Hannah's life that seemed to stand in the way of that call.

How could God choose someone with these debilitating problems as well as paralyzing, claustrophobic fears? Her physical disabilities were not understood or treated with helpful methods for recovery as they are today. Although, like Moses, she had been born into a believing family and was surrounded by God's grace, her whole world changed because God became real to her at age nineteen. Simultaneously, however, she felt altogether inadequate to do the job she seemed called to do.

Throughout Hannah's life, certain circumstances were to bring deliverance and a new perspective on herself and others. She wrote, "It is one of the lovely things about the Master we serve, that he is willing to use in his service dwarfs as well as giants, and feeble folk as well as champions." There is encouragement for all of us in this truth and in the amazing story of this brave woman who broke through her own fears and defied the conventions of her day to bring to many people the Good News.

Hannah would not want us to forget her belief that "there is a great good coming!" In this poem, her friend and colleague John Wood captures the spirit of true expectancy for that "great good" that we continue to look and long for in our own ongoing journey to the High Places.

Do we really believe He is coming again?
That the Lord Jesus Christ will return here to reign?
That the skies with the shout of command will be riven?
And the dead will be raised to the glories of heaven?

Do we really believe that the kings of this world
Will bow in obeisance to Jesus the Lord?
And are we convinced by the power of our faith
That the Spirit will quicken our bodies from death?

As we look at God's Word and reflect on its truths,
Or ponder the "many infallible proofs,"
Our hearts are assured that the One who once died
Will grant us to reign evermore at His side.

So we wait for His coming and watch for its signs,
Discerning the Scripture's prophetic designs,
Observing His purpose unfolding each day,
Preparing our hearts as we walk in His way.

APPENDIX 1 Chronology of Historical Events in Israel Paralleling Life Events of Hannah Hurnard

	PALESTINE/ISRAEL	HANNAH HURNARD
1842	First Anglican bishop, Michael Solomon Alexander (a messianic Jew), arrives in Jerusalem. The following year he founds Christ Church there.	
1905		May 31 Born in Colchester, England
1914–1918	World War I	
1916		Converts to Christianity
1917	Balfour Declaration: Great Britain endorses the establishment of a national home for the Jews in Palestine.	
1918	British Mandate over Palestine begins.	
1920	First Arab anti-Jewish disturbances	
1924		Awakens spiritually and receives missionary call in Keswick, England

PALESTINE/ISRAEL	HANNAH HURNARD
	1926 Graduates from Ridgelands Bible College of Great Britain; mother had died
	1926–1930 Travels with Friends' Evangelistic Band itinerant evangelism team in Ireland and England
	1929 Travels to Palestine with her father and brother
	1932 Begins missionary service as a "gap-filler" in Haifa, Palestine
1936 First formal Arab rebellion against British sympathy to Jews	**1936** Begins evangelism of Jewish settlements; "God's chauffeur" in Haifa until 1947; father marries Marjorie Eady
1937 British commission investigating the Arab rebellion declares Britain's obligations to Arabs and Jews mutually irreconcilable and recommends partition of the country. However, upon further study partition is deemed impractical (1938) and is not pursued.	**1938** Receives call to reach Arab as well as Jewish settlements in Palestine
1939–1945 World War II	

PALESTINE/ISRAEL

1947 *November 29* United Nations' Council votes to partition Palestine into Arab and Jewish states under supervision of the UN Palestine Commission; Great Britain announces that the end of its occupation will be May 14, 1948.

1948 *March* U.S. opposes forcible partition; UN Palestine Commission unable to implement partition due to Arab resistance and lack of British support; *May 14* End of British Mandate in Palestine; *May 15* Birth of the new Jewish state of Israel; siege of Jerusalem by Arab armies begins; *May–December* Arab-Jewish War of Independence; *December 3* "Sincere Truce" in Jerusalem.

1949 *January 25* First general elections in the state of Israel; *January 29* Great Britain recognizes Israel.

HANNAH HURNARD

1948 Missionary housekeeper service at the Jerusalem Mission Hospital completed; remains in Jerusalem

1949 *January* Returns to Essex, England, upon the death of her father; visits Braunwald, Switzerland, where the commission to preach and write comes to her from God; returns to CMJ hospital work in Jerusalem

PALESTINE/ISRAEL

HANNAH HURNARD

1950   Publishes *Watchmen on the Walls* with CMJ (5,000 copies); begins extended writing, speaking, and travel beyond Israel

1951   First speaker, representing CMJ, at Keswick Convention

1952   Ministers in Israel, Essex, and elsewhere; publishes *Hearing Heart* with CMJ

1955   Writes *Hinds' Feet on High Places* while on a six-week vacation in Switzerland

1975   Publishes *Hinds' Feet on High Places* with Tyndale House Publishers, Inc.

1981   Publishes *Eagles' Wings to the Higher Places* with Rahamah Publications

1983   Diagnosed with cancer

1984   Moves permanently to the United States

1988   Publishes *Thou Shalt Remember* with Harper & Row

PALESTINE/ISRAEL

1990 *August* Persian Gulf Crisis begins

1991 *January 17–February 27* Persian Gulf War; *January 17 & 25* Iraq bombs Israel

1993 *September* Israeli–Palestine Liberation Organization (PLO) peace agreement signed

HANNAH HURNARD

1990 *May* Dies at age 84 in Marco Island, Florida

HIGHLIGHTS OF HANNAH HURNARD'S WORKS

"Great Precipice Injury" from Hinds' Feet
on High Places

Much-Afraid stood still and stared. The more she looked, the more stunned she felt. Then she began to tremble and shake all over, for the whole mountain range before her, as far as she could see to left and right, rose up in unbroken walls of rock so high that it made her giddy when she put her head back and tried to look up to the top. The cliffs completely blocked the way before her, yet the path ran right up to them, then stopped. There was no sign of a track in any other direction, and there was no way at all by which the over-hanging, terrifying wall of cliff could be ascended. They would have to turn back.

Just as this overwhelming realization came to her, Suffer-ing caught her hand and pointed to the rocky walls. A hart, followed by a hind, had appeared from among the jumbled rocks around them and were now actually beginning to ascend the precipice.

As the three stood watching, Much-Afraid turned dizzy and faint, for she saw that the hart, which was leading the way, was following what appeared to be a narrow and intensely steep track which went zigzagging across the face of the cliff. In some parts it was only a narrow ledge, in others there appeared to be rough steps, but in certain places she saw that the track appar-ently broke right off.

Then the hart would leap across the gap and go springing upward, always closely followed by the hind, who set her feet exactly where his had been, and leaped after him, as lightly, as sure-footed, and apparently unafraid as it was possible for any creature to be. So the two of them leaped and sprang with perfect grace and assurance up the face of the precipice and disappeared from sight over the top.

Much-Afraid covered her face with her hands and sank down on a rock with a horror and dread in her heart such as she had never felt before. Then she felt her two companions take her hands in theirs and heard them say, "Do not be afraid, Much-Afraid, this is not a dead end after all, and we shall not have to turn back. There is a way up the face of the precipice. The hart and the hind have shown it to us quite plainly. We shall be able to follow it too and make the ascent."

"Oh, no! No!" Much-Afraid almost shrieked. "That path is utterly impossible. The deer may be able to manage it, but no human being could. I could never get up there. I would fall headlong and be broken in pieces on those awful rocks." She burst into hysterical sobbing. "It's an impossibility, an absolute impossibility. I cannot get to the High Places that way, and so can never get there at all." Her two guides tried to say something more, but she put her hands over her ears and broke into another clamor of terrified sobs. There was the Shepherd's Much-Afraid, sitting at the foot of the precipice, wringing her hands and shaking with terror, sobbing over and over again, "I can't do it; I can't. I shall never get to the High Places." Nothing less like royalty could be imagined, but far worse was to follow.

As she crouched on the ground, completely exhausted, they heard a crunching sound and a rattling of loose stones, then a voice close beside her.

"Ha, ha! My dear little cousin, we meet again at last! How

do you find yourself now, Much-Afraid, in this delightfully pleasant situation?"

She opened her eyes in fresh terror and found herself looking right into the hideous face of Craven Fear himself.

"Last Scene on the Mountains of Spices" from **Mountains of Spices**

"Why," she said to herself with a start of surprise, "just see what the King has done. He has made that which seemed the greatest torment and weakness and despair of my life, the thing I most dreaded and suffered from, into the best thing of all. I was always afraid that I must be Craven Fear because of the Fear which so tormented me. He, by his wonderful grace, has changed me into something I could never have hoped to be, a fearless witness. Oh, how wonderful the King is! Oh, what lovely plans and purposes he has, that our greatest torments and failures should become the strongest and best things in our lives. 'Out of weakness he makes us strong to wax valiant in fight and overcome.'"

"No wonder the King loves him," went on Grace and Glory after a moment's pause in her thoughts, and then she gave a happy little laugh. "Why! I can see that already he is champing like a warhorse at the sound of the trumpets to be off to those far-off valleys and to be witnessing there too. All the energy and strength which he used to put into his bullying is now turned into this new service and is become his greatest asset."

Just as she reached this point in her thoughts she saw

Fearless Witness turn to the King and ask a question. Then the King also gave a little laugh, raised his voice and said so clearly that she could hear the words:

"Ask and see what the answer is." Then they both turned and looked around at her as she sat alone in the shade of the great tree.

"Grace and Glory," said the King clearly, "come here to us; we want to speak to you."

Without a moment's hesitation Grace and Glory rose and went and stood beside them, and Peace and Joy walked behind her, taller and more regal and beautiful than ever before.

"Grace and Glory," said Fearless Witness, "we have been talking about those many far-off valleys around the world, where the King needs Fearless Witnesses."

"Yes," said she simply.

"We are going to them," said the King. "Will you go with us?"

Grace and Glory then put one of her hands into his and the other into the hand of Fearless Witness and said, "Make me all that you wish to make me, my Lord, and do with me all that you wish to do."

There the three stood together, the two creatures united with the Creator. He was the will to love, they were the response to that will and the channels through which to express that love.

Then the King's voice rang out clearly and strongly over the Mountain of Aloes, saying with glad assurance and command:

"Ask of me and I will give you the heathen for an inheritance and the uttermost parts of the earth for thy possession" (Ps. 2:8).

Before the three turned to leave the mountain and the ranges of the Mountains of Spices, they sang together a new version of the Jewel Song (Isa. 54:11):

> Here is the sapphire stone!
>   My heart a shining throne
> Where Love himself is crowned as King!
>   Here my obedient will
>   Delights to listen, till
> It knows thy choice in everything.
>
> Here is the agate gem
>   (The fairest Lord of them),
> My ruby stone of blood and flame;
>   Here is my broken heart
>   Made whole, and every part
> Inscribed for ever with thy Name.
>
> Here is the emerald fair,
>   Life breaking everywhere
> Out of the fallen, bruised seed.
>   Here will I praise the Lord,
>   Who hath fulfilled his word
> And given the hundred-fold indeed!
>
> With what fair colors shine
>   These border stones of mine!
> Like royal banners bright, unfurled.
>   Now I go forth, my Lord,
>   Strong through thy mighty word,
> To stake out claims around the world.

"Unity of Love" from Kingdom of Love

"There came a voice out of the cloud saying, 'This is my beloved Son, hear him.' And when the voice was past, Jesus was found alone" (Luke 9:35-36).

"I . . . beseech you that ye walk worthy of the vocation . . . with all lowliness and meekness, with longsuffering, forebearing one another in love; Endeavouring to keep the unity of the Spirit in the bond of peace (Eph. 4:1-3).

. . . What is the real unity of the Body of Christ? How are we to foster and practice it? What is to be our attitude towards those Christians we cannot conscientiously agree with and who, we fear, will lead others into error?

How far ought we to join in cooperation with other Christian groups who do not use our form of worship, or whose methods are different from our own? How should we speak about these differences in teaching and in interpretation to non-Christians? Above all, how should we warn others of danger and engage in combat against real error and denial of our Lord, without doing despite to the Holy Spirit of Love, and damaging ourselves by using destructive thinking? For if destructive habits of thought can work such havoc in the Church of Christ as history records down through the ages, so that even now in this twentieth century we continue to split up and divide into more and more factions and groups all the time, what is the practical healing and uniting principle which we are to practice?

"Ye have left your first love," was the message of the Lord to the first church which began to split and divide up on this very subject of "trying them that say they are prophets, and are not, but are liars" (Rev. 2:2). It seems then the primary

210

cause of disunity is to be found in this, i.e., leaving our first love, not necessarily growing cold and lacking in fervor, but transferring our chief or supreme love to another object, away from Christ himself. Transferring perhaps, our loyalty and warmest love and interest away from the person of Christ to the Church herself? Or our particular section of the Church? Or to sound doctrine, or the faith once delivered to us by the saints?

And in all those cases we immediately find ourselves with a transferred center of combat also, and we shall be versus everybody else who isn't centering on the same object, and like Saul and other really sincere and devout Pharisees, all unknowingly we may even find that we have been fighting against Christ himself.

If the real cause of disunity and weakness in the Church is through having left the first center of love and loyalty, namely, our Lord himself, who is Savior and King and Leader, then the cure for each one of us individually, and corporately, will be to get back to the center we have left. We must get back to our first love and center, the Lord of the Church himself, for even the Church and the doctrines and the gospel itself, take second place to him. And then learn from him to love all our fellow members of his body as he loves them and to behave towards them as he behaves towards us.

For he said, "I have given you an example, that ye should do as I have done to you" (John 13:15). We find over and over again that he continues to give the very blessing, yes, a power to help others to follow him, to many people whom we feel ought not to enjoy those blessings or to have that power, because of their unsound teaching.

If we will but practice the ABC's of love we shall, each one

individually, find the way to loving unity, without uniformity, with all others who are practicing the same principles
of the kingdom of love.

1. Love accepts and loves all who truly love the Lord Jesus
and make him central in their hearts. This attitude puts us
into the relationship of children in one large family, diverse
in temperament, interest, abilities and gifts, work and pas-
times, but all deeply interested in each other and lovingly
ready to help whenever need arises or opportunity occurs,
and never, by any chance, decrying a member of the family
to outsiders. Love accepts with joy. That is the first lovely
principle in the kingdom of love.

There is an interesting account of one of God's servants
listening at a theological college to a professor who was
discrediting the Virgin Birth in one of his lectures, and yet
the professor himself was a sincere and earnest follower of the
Lord Jesus, though intellectually he could not accept that
particular doctrine. As he listened, this servant of God grew
more and more troubled and wretched until he could bear it
no longer, and, lifting his heart to the Lord, he exclaimed
inwardly, "Lord, what is the truth? What am I to believe?
And how can one who professes to love and serve you deny
the Virgin Birth?"

And gently and clearly, it seemed to him, the Lord gave an
answer, which for him was the perfect answer. He said, "I was
born of a virgin, but I accept those who don't see it."

Some glad day we shall all see and understand a great deal
of truth to which we are now quite blind, and then we shall
be very thankful indeed that the Lord did not wait, nor refuse
to accept us, until we could and would understand all that he
meant us to know about him. It was a long time after he

began to follow the Lord that Peter came to understand that he was actually the Son of God as well as beloved Leader and Master.

2. Then love bears all that irks and burdens and disappoints us in those we are put to work with and with whom we find we disagree.

3. And love learns to pray for all such creatively, so that transforming power is liberated in their lives.

If we, as individuals and churches, practice these three principles, and allow love to reign in our hearts and minds, we shall find that our attitude and behavior towards others will be all the time creative of unity and not of distrust and separation. We shall undoubtedly differ in our individual decisions as to how far the Holy Spirit of love means us to go in outward cooperation, but we cannot go wrong in loving. Only love is not in word, but in deed. It does not mean saying with our lips that we do love all the true members of Christ's body, and yet acting as though we heartily disapprove of them and warning others against them. Love must express itself, and seeks for every opportunity to do so.

What sort of unity will be the outcome of creative love thinking and acting? Not an artificial uniformity, but the unity and power which belongs to every individual who practices with other individuals and groups, creative love thinking towards one another, and supreme devotion to our Lord Jesus Christ. Then he will use our witness just as he chooses, and manifest himself to the world through us.

When we have entered into that unity we shall be able to rejoice in quite a new way in the glorious truth that God uses a multitude of other ways and means to help those who have not been able to find help through the things which have been so indescribably helpful to us personally. We shall exult exceedingly over the great multitude which no man can number who have been brought to Christ by others, and in ways which we ourselves could not have followed, and perhaps even though, or in spite of, teaching which we thought was quite erroneous.

In essentials, unity.
In nonessentials, liberty.
In all things, charity.

And perhaps all the great essentials can be summed up in the words spoken by the voice of God from heaven, "This is my beloved Son in whom I am well pleased. Hear him."

"The Wayfarer Leads Us Out" from Wayfarer in the Land

As we sat down to eat our lunch in one of the half-ruined, empty huts on the outskirts of the village, an armed Jewish watchman passed by. He stared at us in some surprise, as most people did on such occasions: two lonely foreign women wandering about together in such troubled times, for the 1936 Arab riots were just starting; then he came up to speak to us.

Sister Patience wore her distinctive Deaconess uniform, and after staring at us for a moment, this young watchman said in a friendly tone of voice "You must be missionaries. Have you any Christian literature I can read?" And once again we found a soul who had been brought into touch with Christians in the past and was glad to hear more about their Lord.

We found this unaccustomed work of visiting in the villages extremely tiring, all the more so because we had to experiment all the time in order to find the best way of setting about it. But very quickly we got into the habit of waiting upon God, before ever we went out, for his guidance as to which village he would have us visit. We did not work out a methodical plan, and after crossing out each place visited, say, "This is the next on our list; we will go there next time," but we spread the survey map out before us and studied the different names and positions of the places and then definitely asked that we might be led to real assurance as to which we were to visit next.

Also whenever we went out we used to stop the car some distance away from the place we were going to, for prayer, and in order to claim that the door would be open for us, and that we might be led to individuals whose hearts had already been prepared in some way.

I mention this because experience has led me to believe that this is a more practical and successful way of going about such work, than a cut-and-dried plan, however methodically it may be prepared. It is better to trust the Holy Spirit to lead us to those he knows are ready for our coming, than to parcel out a village, so many houses to be visited and so many streets to be finished in a certain time. Also it seems to me that in such work we should be very adaptable and ready to modify or change at a moment's notice any part of the arrangement, as the Holy Spirit may prompt, rather than to insist on adhering rigidly to the original plan.

Often we have driven slowly right through a village, praying that the Lord would make us sure which street to stop in, and have perhaps turned back and retraced our steps to one special street and there found a particularly needy soul awaiting us. And we have been amazed at the many hungry, dissatisfied hearts with whom we came in contact, and the many who through recent sorrow, bereavement, illness, or other family troubles, were conscious of their need of some refuge and of more than human help.

Another point which we also made a special matter for prayer, was that the Lord would make us more skillful in winning the interest and confidence of the people as soon as the door was opened, so that we might get inside the house and have the opportunity for a real talk, undisturbed by the curious stares of passersby. It seemed to us that a few really earnest talks inside a house, when individuals would speak to us of their own religious experience, or complete lack of it, and confess their deepest needs, was far more worthwhile than scattering literature at a far larger number of houses, though that is very worthwhile work too.

We prayed earnestly therefore that we might develop a better technique of approach, and we found that by far the most likely means of being invited into a house was a friendly smile and a courteous and kind greeting, and some appreciative remark if possible, about the garden or the building, or a sympathetic inquiry about obvious difficulties, such as the lack of water, miserable condition of the road, or lonely situation of the village. We learned to keep on the alert for points of friendly contact, and have come to feel certain that a stiff, reserved manner, or dogmatic patronizing tone of voice, will bar the door quicker than anything else, while a friendly smile and easy natural greeting will often effect wonders.

I am not of course forgetting that an easy natural manner is the one thing the novice at such works feels that she is never likely to acquire, but the fact is, as we have seen again and again, the shyest and most awkward can achieve it as a result of humble, believing prayer, and an earnest desire to forget oneself altogether, and to think only of the need and spiritual poverty of those being visited.

On the other hand it may be necessary later on to keep a sharp check on oneself in order to avoid going to the opposite extreme, rushing into insincere gushing or flattery. This can be a very real snare, as I well remember discovering on one occasion when we were trying to get into the house of a very fanatical old lady, whose cottage was in a terribly neglected and dirty condition.

She was pouring out a torrent of abuse against us, and while this was going on, I noticed a particularly ugly and crude piece of embroidery hanging on the wall just inside the door, and when she paused for breath, I said, as sweetly as possible (being loath to turn away unsuccessful), "What a beautiful piece of embroidery you have there. I wonder if I may be allowed to look at it."

Far from being mollified however, she swung around on me and shouted, "Now don't you try to get round me in that way, you hypocrite! You know as well as I do that you are not the least interested in it." I knew this thoroughly served me right, and felt very properly rebuked.

I mention all these points in passing, as we ourselves learned everything in the hard school of experience, and passed through many stages of experiment and lack of success. We discovered pitfalls by falling into them, and came to realize the better ways of approach only after sorrowing over bad ones. But there is no reason why other novices at such work, warned by our experience, should not avoid these mistakes from the very beginning.

"The Wayfarer Teaches Us to Fish for Men" *from* Wayfarer in the Land

In the late afternoon, we were able to bump thankfully back along the camel track to the safety of the main road, very plentifully besmeared with evidences of our recent adventure.

We were soon faced with a new challenge to faith, and a job which both of us shrank from in real fear. A large village remained unvisited in our area, where the people were notably more orthodox than any others, and belonged to the strictest sect of their religion. We would gladly have missed this place altogether, but the more we prayed about it, the more clearly the answer seemed to come, "Go preach the gospel to every creature," and the need must include the orthodox and fanatical as well as the more easy-going.

The day came when all the villages had been reached except this one, and two or three others, which . . . seemed even more formidable and alarming than the one before us.

I can still remember the ghastly feeling, somewhere in the pit of my stomach, as we approached the side road which would lead us to this orthodox settlement. Quite automatically I decreased speed until we were only crawling along. Neither of us spoke a word. I dared not tell Peace how frightened I was for fear of making her feel worse, and she was silent for the same reason.

We stopped the car just outside the village and had our usual time of prayer, and then as the inevitable must be faced, we started off again and drove into the village. Here I was so literally inhibited by fright that I could not stop the car, and we drove straight through the village and out again on the other side, and only came to a standstill when all the houses were left behind.

So we had some more prayer and turned round and drove into the village again, and as good as repeated the maneuver, only just as we were crawling out on the first side we had entered by, Peace said, "Let's turn left up this street where there are only a few houses, and start there." This we did, but even so I drove right along the street without stopping and only the fact that it proved to be a blind alley, prevented us from leaving the village in yet a third direction. When at last the road came to an abrupt end, we stopped and climbed out.

I have only a confused recollection of what happened then. Evidently our initial entry into the village, and departure, and mysterious return, had aroused interest. Also some boys quickly gathered round the car and spotted our bags of books. They inquired who we were and why we had come, and, despair making us bold, we answered with the bald statement that we were Christian missionaries and had brought literature with us. Whereupon, though we were too nervous to notice it, the little boys dispersed in all directions.

We then made our way up to the first house, and a man wearing the traditional garments indicating his strict orthodoxy, met us at the door. As we stood talking to him and showing our books, the astounding thing happened. People began hurrying towards us from all directions, and as they came up they clamored for our books and Scripture portions. Again and again we explained that we were Christians and these were Christian books, and still they clamored. Then Peace, unable to restrain her astonishment said, "But I thought you were all very orthodox Jews. Why do you want these books about the Christ?"

219

And somebody answered immediately, "Outwardly we are orthodox, but inwardly we are dissatisfied."

One special person stands out in my hazy memory of that three-quarters of an hour. A very frail old man painfully pushed his way through the crowd and clutched my arm. "Give me one of those books" he quavered, and pointed to the last Hebrew New Testament which remained, and for which so many were clamoring that I did not know whom to choose. He was old and pathetically frail, and my heart smote me. All his long life evidently he had lived according to the strictest traditions of his religion. Now he surely could not understand what he was asking for. If he took this book into his hands he would be defiled.

He had always supposed that it was a blasphemous book and that he should spit at every mention of the One about whom it spoke. How could I let him unwittingly touch a book by which he would afterwards feel that he had been made unclean. He plucked my arm again beseechingly, and I said as gently as possible, "I think perhaps you do not know what this book is. It is the New Testament, and is all about Jesus Christ."

"Yes, yes," he said impatiently, "I understand that. For many years I have wanted to read this book, but never found a copy." And as I placed it in his hand he opened it and held it under his short-sighted eyes and without a word turned away, reading as he went, and taking no further notice of anyone. . . .

Stones began to rattle on the roof and walls, and although the Rabbi went to the door and tried to still the rabble, we found that all the responsible adults had left, and only the boys remained. They paid no heed to his request that they should disperse, and it was quite obvious that a quiet talk would be impossible.

As it was plain there was no opportunity for us to visit quietly from house to house, I decided that I would try and draw off the crowd of boys, and leave Peace and our friend to talk with the Rabbi. So I opened the door and slipped out, and as an instant's hush fell, I said with a cheerfulness which I was far from feeling, that if they would follow me I would be glad to answer any questions about ourselves and the purpose of our visit, that they cared to ask. To my great relief the ruse succeeded. They closed in around me, evidently glad to have a visible target for their abuse, and I led the way to an open grassy slope just outside the Rabbi's garden, in sight of the house and car, but far enough away to insure comparative quiet for the friends inside the house.

I sat down on a rock, and about twenty boys between the ages of eight and sixteen gathered around. They began shouting questions at me, but as I was quite miraculously able to maintain a quiet and smiling demeanor, they very quickly quieted down. First they plied me with a lot of simple questions about their Torah, and seemed surprised when I answered them all correctly, and thus revealed a knowledge of the book quite unexpected in a Christian.

Somewhat mollified, they quieted still more. Then one of them picked up a large stone and announced that he was going to smash my watch, as their holy book said that all unbelievers were accursed and should be treated as badly as possible. I replied with surprise that in a careful study of their book I had never come across any such statement, but on the contrary, I thought they were exhorted to show courtesy and hospitality to strangers who sought their help and protection and to follow the example of their father Abraham. I asked him to give me chapter and verse in support of his statement, and everybody laughed and he sheepishly dropped the stone.

But they were not yet satisfied. One of them pointed to a stone lying on the ground and said, "That's your God, you Christians worship stones." Another cried out "No, this is their God," and placed two sticks on the ground in the shape of a cross, and then ground his heel on the sticks and spat. And yet a third laughed and pointed to a village dog, slinking on the outskirts of the crowd, and shouted, "No, their God is a dog, look at him over there."

A curious thing happened as I sat there on the rock, listening to their mockery and looking at their laughing faces. The inner nervousness all went and a quite unexpected surge of longing and a desire to help them filled me. The ringleader who had done most of the catechizing, was about fourteen years old, with black hair and flashing eyes, and a bold, easy way of quelling the others, when he wanted to speak himself. As I watched him so eagerly standing up for his own religion, and trying to demonstrate the badness of mine, I was reminded of young Saul of Tarsus, and then I pictured this boy as a disciple of Jesus Christ, and just as earnestly defending his faith in him.

And then the crowd of faces all staring at me no longer belonged to a rabble of hooligans, but to a crowd of Jewish boys who had never once had the opportunity of hearing about the Savior. And who could say when they would hear if I said nothing now. I pictured the Lord Jesus himself sitting on the rock and talking to them in his own wonderful way, and how quickly he would have won them. And then I lifted my heart in an earnest prayer that he would take my mouth and mind and say something to them through me.

Then I said haltingly in Hebrew and groping for the right words, "No, the God I worship is not a stone, nor a cross of wood, nor a dog. Let me tell you a little about him."

I think they must have sensed how earnestly I wanted to tell them for they hushed and listened, and even helped me out with the Hebrew words when I got stuck, and though it was desperately little that I could say, they grew very friendly, and at last asked me for some portions of the Scriptures. I smiled and said, "I am afraid you will tear them up."

But the ringleader said, "No, give them to me. I know who will read them and who will tear them."

I handed him a gospel, and two or three voices shouted, "Tear it up." "It's vile," but he thrust it under his ragged shirt, and smiled at me reassuringly, and said, "Don't be afraid. I won't tear it or let anyone else do so."

"God's Kingdom Is Here" from Walking Among the Unseen

Once there was a little boy (so the story goes) who lived in a house on the top of a hill. One morning when he ran outside to go down the hill to school, he stopped dead in his tracks and stared—for there, on the top of a hill on the other side of the valley, he saw a house with windows made of gleaming gold, flashing in the sunshine like an enchanted palace in a fairy tale. Where had it come from? How did it get there? Who lived in it? What fortunate people they must be to have glorious golden windows instead of ordinary glass ones! What wonderful treasures there must be inside such a mansion.

All that day he couldn't fix his attention on anything else. When at last school was over, he decided that instead of going straight home, he would climb the other hill and visit the house with the golden windows.

So off he went, and climbed and climbed until at last he reached the top of the hill. He looked around eagerly for the house he had seen. But there was nothing there but an ordinary house, and a kind-faced woman standing at the garden gate with a little girl about his own age beside her.

Panting and perspiring but full of eagerness, he asked the woman where the house with the golden windows was to be found. She looked very surprised and said, "There is no such house on this hilltop. Indeed, ours is the only one and, as you can see, it has ordinary glass windows." Then seeing how dreadfully crestfallen and disappointed he looked, she said kindly, "Never mind! Come inside and I will give you and my little girl a glass of lemonade each, and a piece of cake, and you can eat it together in the garden."

So the children sat together in the garden until it was evening and time for him to go home, and he poured out to the little girl all about the entrancing house which he had seen. Certainly it must have been a fairy one, for apparently it could appear and disappear. Oh, what fortunate people must own it, and how disappointed he was not to have found it, but he was determined to look for it every day until he could find it at last.

The little girl listened with wide-open, understanding eyes, nodding her head from time to time, and when he had finished she said mysteriously, "Well, there really is a house with golden windows, though Mommy doesn't know about it. But I have seen it, too, and it's just splendid. Only it isn't on this hilltop but on another one. Come with me and I will show you."

They went together to the garden gate and the little girl pointed and truly, there, away on another hilltop, there was a house with glorious flashing golden windows, so dazzling that the boy kept blinking his eyes as he looked at them.

"Isn't it beautiful!" said the little girl wistfully. "Oh, how I wish that I could live in a house with golden windows, for I am sure that they must look out onto a beautiful fairy world instead of this ordinary one!"

Then the little boy, still staring incredulously, exclaimed, "But that's my house. There are the two big pine trees, one on each side of the house, and I can see my mother taking the laundry off the clothesline."

Then, as they both stared in amazement, the sun sank a little lower and one by one the shining golden windows disappeared as they no longer reflected its rays, and the house became just the ordinary, safe, happy little home which he knew so well. His mother must be wondering anxiously where he had gone, and he must go home at once. So he said "Good-bye" to the little girl, promising to return to play with her again, and ran down the hill and up the other, and told his mother the whole curious story. When he had finished, she smiled at him lovingly and said, "Well, you know, I really do believe that we are very fortunate, and that we do live in a house with golden windows, because the love of God comes shining into them each day, and it is that which makes us so happy together and makes ordinary things bring us so much joy. If you understand this you will find, as Daddy and I have done, that we do live in a world more beautiful and wonderful than any fairyland, because we let God help us to make good and happy things happen instead of sad and bad ones, and you will learn to help us make them too."

I read the story about the house with the golden windows when I was a little girl, and that is a long time ago. But as the years have passed, and in a special way quite recently, I too have become one of "the fortunate people," and I too live in a house with golden windows—and doors—opening out, not into an unreal fairy story world, but into the glorious world of the Kingdom of God, filled with good and beautiful things and where blessed and happy things happen, because I have been fortunate enough to learn the secret of letting God make everything in it. As he is the creator of very good things, it becomes happier and more fortunate all the time!

To some, my life is ordinary and typical. But because God is in it, it is actually exciting and always new. It has golden windows.

"Love" from God's Transmitters

"Our Father which art in heaven." The desire to be kept continually in the attitude of child-like love and trust and delight in the Father's presence. To be utterly dependent on him, and utterly like him. To live in heaven even while here on earth, for heaven is the realm where everyone thinks and expresses the creative love-thoughts of the heavenly Father.

"Hallowed be thy name." The desire to share in the nature of Holy Love himself. To be completely separated (which is the meaning of hallowed) from every thought which is not in

harmony with holy love. Passionate thankfulness for the glorious truth, that the name and nature of God is love.

"Thy Kingdom come; thy will be done on earth as it is done in heaven." The desire that the kingdom of God should be established in every human heart, so that Love shall reign on earth even as he does in heaven. A consuming desire to cooperate in every way possible in bringing this to pass.

"Give us this day our daily bread." This surely is a hunger and desire of mind as well as of body, a longing for communion with God himself, that we may be fed by him in soul as well as in body. The desire to receive from him that which will strengthen us, and cause us to grow spiritually. "For man doth not live by bread alone, but by every word which proceedeth out of the mouth of God" (Matt. 4:3).

"And forgive us our debts as we forgive our debtors." The longing desire of the heart both to be forgiven, and to be able to forgive, and thus be made like our Redeemer; able to transmit God's life to others.

"And lead us not into temptation, but deliver us from evil." A desire to be kept recoiling from every thought of evil, a yearning to be kept holy; separated from all that is unlike God. A longing to be strengthened to cut off all that we know has the power to tempt us and incline us to thoughts which are contrary to holy love.

"For thine is the kingdom, the power and the glory, for ever and ever, Amen." The desire to be kept in an attitude of heart and

mind which adores and magnifies and praises the God of love continually, which goes through each day praising God for everything. The desire to be kept from entertaining a single murmuring or complaining or self-pitying thought, and that Love himself shall be the center and object of all praise, for ever and for ever.

May these seven desires, which sum up the perfect desires of our Lord's own heart, and his own attitude and habits of thought, be realized in us also. For as long as this is the attitude of our hearts, we may be joyfully sure that we are abiding in him, and so are able to receive and transmit God's thoughts of creative love, without any effort or struggle or strain on our part.

Undoubtedly God, who so loves variety (as he has revealed in his creative activities) and who appears to be so uninterested in uniformity, will use his children's thought lives in very different ways. Probably he has different thought ministries for each of us. Some may be called to wrestle in prayer, and some to make spiritual discoveries and think his thoughts after him in a great variety of ways. But if we are abiding in our Lord and Savior, the lovely truth is evident that all our thoughts of love and goodwill and longing to help others, of pity and understanding sympathy and compassion, are a form of intercession, for these thoughts are broadcast and transmitted to those whom God yearns to help and save and bless.

We pray without ceasing when all our thoughts are under the control of the Holy Spirit, whether we think them when we are on our knees in our own rooms, or at the communion table, or in the kitchen, or office, or business store, in the bus or train or on the street. For intercession is not primarily our hearts pleading with God, but God transmitting his power through us.

"Love in Oneness" from Winged Life

Love is wonderfully creative. God is love, and God is the Creator of all, and love is the only really creative power in the universe.

Here is a common, everyday illustration of the creativity of love, to illustrate why we need it, and the harm and the damage we do to each other when we withhold it. Have you not noticed that if you meet someone who dislikes you, and they refuse to smile at you and even scowl or cross the street or look the other way, how quickly there awakens and stirs in you a feeling of resentment or pain or answering dislike? That person has created in you the same feelings which are in their own heart.

If you have to work in the presence of someone who actively dislikes or despises you, even though they may not often express it in words, how it paralyzes and cripples you and brings out all the worst that is in you. Have you ever found yourself really helped by someone you know dislikes you? Or able to respond quickly to a Christian who has felt led to speak to you on some matter, for your own good, when you know and feel that one disapproves of you, or despises you, and is only speaking because their feelings are so jarred by you that they are determined they must change you? No, you cannot be helped by that person. Indeed, they rather hinder than help you.

In the same way, however, if you meet someone in the street or the train who smiles at you and greets you as though they were really glad to see you, or expresses some gracious and kindly interest in you, how instantly creative such an attitude is. Joy awakens in you, you feel stirred on to greater efforts, and something comes to life in you that you were not conscious of before. Are not the friends who help you, the ones who love you in spite of your faults, and who do not allow those faults to make any difference in their love to you, so that they do not get exasperated and infuriated with you? These are the disciples who share the creative power of their Lord.

Of course it is so. Love is creative, and dislike and lack of love are destructive and we feel this (almost unconsciously) the whole time. Thus, when we refuse to love, and when we ignore and disdain others, it is not just a negative attitude. We are doing them actual harm, for unless they are garrisoned by love themselves and know the secret of the Lord and are actively loving us as he has taught them to, there will awaken in them active dislike and ill will.

Then arises another great question. How can we love the unlovely and the sin-marred, the altogether unattractive, even the criminal and the vicious? How can we possibly desire to feel one with them? Indeed, ought we even to desire to do so? Surely love cannot love the unlovely and those who are antagonistic to love?

The answer, of course, is to be found in the Lord Jesus, incarnate Love himself. How did he solve this problem? How did he react to the unlovely and to the enemies of love?

By becoming incarnate in fallen mankind; making himself the actual representative of the hideous, sin-blemished and sin-deformed human race. "God commendeth his love towards us in that, while we were yet sinners, Christ died for us." Christ insisted, as man, in realizing his oneness with us all while we were yet sinners.

Then can the Lord of love really love the unlovely? Alter the question by one word and let each of us ask ourselves, "Can the Lord of love really love me? For I am so unlovely and sin-defiled." What can he possibly see to like, much less to love, in you and me, confirmed breakers as we are, of his perfect and royal law of love?

Can he love us, we who are so selfish, ugly and blemished, with so many unlovely habits? Yes, we know he does. How does he love us? When we understand that we shall be able to understand how he can help us to love the unlovely and to realize our oneness with even the most unattractive.

The answer is that he looks upon us with an infinite compassion. He sees us as a race of people hideously disfigured and deformed by a loathsome disease; he sees the whole body of mankind corrupted and sick and dying. "The whole head is sick and the whole heart faint. From the sole of the foot even unto the head there is no soundness in it, but wounds and bruises and putrifying sores: they have not been closed, neither bound up, neither mollified with ointment" (Isa. 1:5-6).

He knows, too, that we cannot help ourselves, for we were born into this corrupted and diseased human race. In some people the horrible symptoms of sin are appallingly evident; in others, who are still young and outwardly lovely, there may be apparent only a few little blemishes, but these reveal to the great Physician the presence of the same awful disease. He sees us as sick unto death, and has compassion upon us, for he said:

"They that are whole need not a physician, but they that

are sick." "The Son of Man is come to seek and to save that which is lost."

Surely, we who are followers of the Lord of love and members of his Body, do need a revolution in our understanding of sin and in our attitude to these multitudes of men and women and little children who, like ourselves, have all been born with an incurable disease, greatly sinned against as well as sinning against others, and who are utterly unable to cure themselves.

"Would you," says Doctor Alexander Whyte, "hate or strike back at a blind man who stumbled against you in the street? Or retaliate at a maniac on his way to the madhouse? And shall we retaliate on a miserable man driven mad with diabolical passion or diseased with ill will?"

All visible sins in men and women are symptoms manifesting this deadly disease, and they should awaken in us infinite compassion as well as horror.

The great Physician "is able to have compassion on . . . them that are out of the way" (Heb. 5:2). "When he saw the multitudes he was moved with compassion on them" (Matt. 9:36). "For God sent not his Son into the world to condemn the world; but that the world through him might be saved" (John 3:17).

Nowhere in the gospel does our Lord and Savior condemn sinners, though he warns continually. His denunciations and condemnations were all spoken to those who saw and beheld him—the great Physician and his power to heal the sin-sick and to save the fallen, and who refused to be healed themselves. It was to professedly religious people that he spoke of condemnation, to those who had light and rejected it; and to those who refused to confess that they were among the

232

sin-sick and who rejected the cure which he offered them at such incredible cost to himself. "This," said he, "is the condemnation, that light is come into the world, and men love darkness rather than light" (John 3:19).

This is the condemnation, the only condemnation that he uttered, and he spoke it to the religious leaders of Israel before whose very eyes he was manifested as the light of the world.

If we, too, desire to realize our oneness with sinners and to love them creatively as Christ loved us, then our whole thought attitude towards them may need to be changed. The eyes of our understanding must be opened so that we shall be able to see them (even the unloveliest of them) in their hopeless need and misery as sin-sick and diseased unto death. Then all that is foul and ugly and unclean (or merely unattractive) will awaken in us a passionate desire to share, if possible, in bringing about their healing and transformation through the saving power of Christ.

"Witness to a Miracle" from Watchmen on the Walls

All normal and accustomed Mission work was coming to an end, but witnesses were still needed who would live among the Jewish people. The dry bones of Israel were to experience two phases, a coming together in union as a Nation, bound together with flesh and sinews. Then the second stage must certainly follow, a quickening into spiritual life and power.

"There was a noise and behold a shaking, and the bones came together, bone to his bone . . . but there was no breath in them. Then said He unto me, Prophesy unto the Wind

233

and say 'Come from the four winds O Breath, and breathe upon those slain that they may live.' So I prophesied as He commanded me, and the Breath came into them, AND THEY LIVED, and stood up upon their feet, an exceeding great army" (Ezek. 37:9-10).

Morning after morning I pondered these verses and prayed for an understanding heart, and found myself asking, "Is this really His Word to me? His promise? Have we really reached this stage? Are we actually so honoured as to be His witnesses among Israel in these last weeks or months or years which are to see their revival? Are we the intercessors who are to pray to the Wind of Heaven, 'Come O Breath and breathe upon these slain that they may live?'"

At that time I am sure very few non-Jews thought that Israel would be able to stand against the invading armies and drive them out of the land. I myself did not expect that the Jewish State would come so soon into being and achieve success. I supposed that the Jewish people, while still in unbelief, would be unable in their own strength to bring to pass such a miracle. It was this expectation which made the thought of staying in the Jewish area while the Arabs achieved success such a nightmare, but by the end of those few days, I was sure that God meant me to remain, so wonderful, glorious, and certain did the Word seem as He spoke it, day by day, on that quiet hillside that at the time nothing seemed impossible. I felt neither fear nor shrinking, only an awed wonder and joy in the thought of being privileged to remain with others in "The Valley of Dry Bones" and at such a time, to pray for the Breath of Life to come to them.

But it was all very different when I came down from the

"mountain top," and looked at things from the earthly angle again. Even before I left Nablus we heard that the Mandatory Government was going to broadcast to the British Community urging all Britishers to leave Palestine before the end of the Mandate, and undertaking to provide facilities for their departure. At first several hundred British civilians and business men had expected to remain in Jerusalem, but already it was widely believed among the Jewish people that once the Mandate was given up Britain meant to support the Arab cause, and in that case, all Britains would be enemies, and surely the Jewish Authorities would not tolerate any of them remaining in the Jewish area. What was the good of imagining that God was telling me to stay in Jewish Jerusalem if the Jews would never permit it? And then I was constantly tormented by my imagination, picturing all the horrors that lay ahead, the siege, the breaking through of the Arab armies, the capture of the Jewish area, and the wiping out of the inhabitants. It would mean, I supposed, being cut off from all communication with the outside world, separated from friends and fellow missionaries, under constant fire, suspected by the Jews, and perhaps imprisoned, unable to get out even if I wanted to, I who so loved open spaces and being alone with freedom to move about. The more I thought about these things the more impossible it seemed. Perhaps God was only testing me to see if I was ready to do His will, and after submitting to His guiding, would lead me to remain in the Arab area, perhaps at the Mission Station in the Old City, with the rest of the staff. There we would not be besieged and would have a back door open into Transjordan. But there, written down plainly in the little book I use in my

Quiet Times, was the message I felt so sure He had given me during those mornings when I went alone to meet Him, asking to be shown His will. Had it all been a mistake? Or was it really the Word of the Lord? Anyhow I knew that the horrible pictures I was tempted to see in imagination were in all probability attempts by the Enemy to get me out of the line of the Lord's will, just as he had so often done in the past.

> "Better hath He been for years,
>   Than thy fears."

were the words which came to my mind as they had so often done before, bringing me great comfort.

On April the 10th [1948] I returned to Jerusalem. . . . Then I heard the dreadful news that during the night a band of Jewish terrorists had raided the nearby village of Deir Yassin. . . .

It was terribly difficult during these months to free one's mind from bitterness and the all-prevailing atmosphere of hate. Things were happening on all sides which shocked one to the heart, and one must remember that all reports from both sides were inclined to be distorted, or at least to leave out extenuating circumstances, or the reasons which led to such actions. And one needs to remember, too, that the names "Terrorist" and "Patriot" may be applied to the very same persons, depending entirely upon one's own point of view. Undoubtedly there were many on both sides who carried out these dreadful acts of violence who were heroic and sincere patriots, longing to liberate their people from foreign interference and to gain possession of Palestine for their own people, Arabs or Jews as the case may be.

But the frightful thing about any victory achieved by violence and force is the legacy of hate which it leaves behind,
and the seeds sown for further unleashing of strife and
bloodshed.

When I got back after those days of holiday in Nablus, I
found that plans were well under way for helping the Hebrew
Christians to leave the country. It looked as though no
missionaries would be left in the Jewish area at all, and that
if they did stay there would be no Hebrew Christian congre-
gation left for them to minister to. The food situation was
becoming dreadful, and it seemed unlikely that rations would
be spared to anyone but Jews, and that no one would be
allowed to remain unless they were willing to help the war
effort. Deep down in my heart I heaved a sigh of relief. It
seemed that not only would I not be expected to stay in the
Jewish area, but would not be allowed to do so. As I tried to
push on one side what the Lord had said on the hillside at
Nablus, deep down, in the innermost recess of my being, my
will cried out longingly, "Don't let me miss Thy will, Lord.
Thou knowest that I trust Thee to make and keep me
willing."

One day after lunch we had coffee in the sunny courtyard,
and as I went upstairs to my room, I was thinking with a half
guilty satisfaction that after all I would be able to remain
there at the Mission House and be near the food market, and
perhaps still be free to drive around, and if the worst came to
the worst, retire to Transjordan. Suddenly an agonising un-
rest seized me, the most dreadful mental disquiet. I remembered my Lord's words at Nablus and His call to live among
the Jews as a witness. He had offered me the honour of being
one of His Watchmen, and here I was trying to evade and

wriggle out of it. I said to myself again, "But we can't any of us live in the Jewish areas. The Authorities won't allow it." Then in a dreadful flash I remembered Gideon's fleece, and the sign that God gave him that he was in God's will and not imagining his call. The Lord seemed to say, "If the Authorities will give you permission to remain, are you willing to do so? That will be your fleece. Ruth told you yesterday that if it were possible she, too, would choose to stay in the Jewish area and try to carry on the Girls' School. If the permission is granted, will you take it that that is what I want you both to do?"

The inner struggle became so unbearable I went up on the roof top alone, and the Enemy pressed sore against me, in what seemed an overwhelming attack. I felt an agony of dread and pain and horror. I couldn't do this thing. I couldn't voluntarily go and live in a besieged area, with no one knew what horrors ahead, and no way of escape. For a little while it was all pain, but thank God not a moment of rebellion. While my flesh cried out that I couldn't do it, my heart said, "I delight to do Thy will, O my God."

"On the True High Places" from Lessons Learned on the Slopes of the High Places

Written during a three-week visit to Switzerland on my way back to Israel after a short visit to England following the death of my father and the winding up of his affairs. I had said farewell, as I thought, to the old home in which I had been born and where I had been welcomed back by my father on all my furloughs from missionary work in the Middle East.

Come Up to Me into the Mount
Braunwald Monday, May 23, 1949

"And the Lord said . . . , Come up to me into the mount. . . . And a *cloud* covered the *mount*. And the glory of the Lord abode upon [the] *mount*. . . . And the *cloud* covered it six days; and the seventh day he called unto Moses out of the midst of the *cloud*. . . . And the Lord spake" (Exod. 24:12, 15, 16; 25:1).

Through mist and cloud and by a strange path where I could never see more than one step at a time, the Lord has brought me here to Switzerland, "to a high mountain apart." I believe that he will speak to me out of the cloud; for I know he has something to say, and I long to hear it.

Three days ago as I came up in the funicular railway from Linthal to Braunwald, in Glarus, there was such thick mist and cloud that nothing at all was visible. Not a chalet nor tree nor wall could be seen, and even the Bergfrieden Deaconess House was quite invisible until we reached the door!

The sisters said that for over a week it had been very like that, and it might continue in the same way for weeks longer. Humanly speaking, it was very disappointing to come to Switzerland after so many years' absence, and be unable to see anything.

But that evening from my window in the huge wooden chalet I saw one patch of rocky precipice and snow exposed for a few moments through the driving rain and mist. I had been told that the snow mountains rise in a glorious range just the other side of the valley, but I could never have guessed so from what was visible.

Next morning I awoke at 4:30 A.M., and there the mountains were! How right those people are who say that one

239

might just as well not come to Switzerland unless one is prepared to rise before the sun! Now the mountains appeared. Still lying in bed, I saw them through the uncurtained window—their tops still buried in the cloud—but a glorious snow and rock range rising like a wall just across the narrow valley. All that day the mist was clearing, but the *clouds* remained low and still hid most of the view.

Today I awoke at 5:00 A.M., and lo! Clear and rosy in the dawn light against a background of calm blue sky were the High Places I so longed to see.

Now I am sitting on a huge green slope, starred with tiny blue gentians, and the buttercups are scattered like gold all around me. This is the Braunwald Alp, and the snow mountains rise like walls on three sides of it. I sit here and look out on beauty beyond expression. To the right is an immense cliff over which the Brumbach waterfall leaps down with a noise "of many waters." Opposite me is a mountain with huge rock walls and seven peaks rising one above the other. Beside them, though not quite so high, is another peak shaped like a horn. This seven-crested mountain is the Ortstock and the horn is called Hoher Turm. This is the mountain that dominates the scene in Braunwald, and it is more picturesque than any of the other neighboring giants.

To the left rise great ramparts and ranges of snow and rock. While I sit here in brilliant sunshine, an immense dark cloud has overshadowed the heights, and I hear a distant peal of thunder. . . .

The Brumbach Falls

The whole neighborhood is filled with the sound of rushing water pouring down over and between the rocks. For me, the two falls, the Brumbach and the Zillbach, are like two glorious angels of love, leaping down from the heights to carry life and power to the valleys far below.

O my Lord! What do you want to say to me today? Help me to hear your voice. Teach me to understand the language spoken by your creation all around me. Help me to receive into my innermost soul the great truth that, "To whom much is given, of them shall much be required."

Lifting my eyes, I look across the valley at the Brumbach falls and see the water pouring itself down in an extraordinary ecstasy of self-abandoned giving—and I know now that is my Lord's message to me.

I have asked him to help me to understand the language of this book of nature. And the first message and lesson his creation utters is this one. It is so clear that I do understand it. It speaks of love's eternal, ecstatic joy in ceaseless, blissful giving.

1. The first characteristic of true love is *humility:* the pouring of oneself down lower and lower in self-effacement and self-denial. The message of running water always is, "Go lower. Find the lowest place. That is the only way to true fulfillment."

2. The next characteristic of love is *giving.* The poured-out life gives life and power to others. The more love gives, the more it fulfills itself. "For it is Love's prerogative to GIVE and GIVE and GIVE."

3. The third characteristic of love is *service.* The Brumbach falls, in the act of giving themselves, serve the whole valley and far beyond it. The water means a supply of irrigation, electricity, and light for many, many homes, gardens, and orchards. To be utterly abandoned to the goal of

giving oneself to others, and going down lower, is the joy and ecstasy of love.

"Perfect love casteth out fear." Yes, that is what the water utters so exultingly as it rushes toward the great, terrifying rocky lip of the gorge and plunges over, utterly abandoned and unafraid of the dreadful depths into which it must fall, down onto the threatening rocks below.

Watching the waters as they leap over the edge, and following them with my eyes as they fall downward, I discover that the whole movement is one of the most breathtaking examples of utter rejoicing and of triumphant, almost delirious abandonment that I have ever seen. If one looks at the falls as a whole, they are marvelously beautiful. But if one gazes at one particular part of the water as it plunges over the lip, and then watches it as it falls right down, the almost crazy, blissful abandonment is staggering. I never saw motion so utterly expressive of joy! The movement looks like perfect rapture, fearless surrender to a hitherto unknown delight, the greatest it is possible to experience. The downward motion is light, adventurous, and perfectly happy. The water, after casting itself over the rocks, seems to be held up and supported as though floating down on wings! A glorious contradiction indeed.

How can one abandon oneself in this way? Well, the scene before me answers this question.

The falls come down from the *heights*. Before they can do that there must first come the experience of "He maketh my feet like hinds' feet, and setteth me upon my high places" (Ps. 18:33).

One cannot get a mighty and powerful *fall* of water if there is only a low place and a short way for it to fall. It is the "high places" of faith and obedience which make the falls of love possible!

The Ortstock, the great seven-pinnacled mountain opposite, is a wonderful picture of spiritual experience, rising from height to height and peak to peak. The summits of the "high places" are the powerhouses from which love pours itself down in joyful surrender. One can never truly love until by faith and surrendered obedience one reaches the "high places" and there learns to go "skipping and leaping" on the mountains of difficulty as though they were "an asphalt road"!

Everything around me seems to be designed to emphasize this lesson. I have been brought to a place where all God's creation appears to be uttering things in a language which only becomes clearly audible and understood by hearts that have been learning in the school of suffering. It is the language which one begins to spell out in one's innermost soul when one is on a cross to which self is being transfixed by nails of pain and anguish of heart. It compares to the experiences in the Siege of Jerusalem, and the years in terrorist-ridden Palestine which led up to this past year, 1948. . . .

The Torrent
Braunwald May 25, 1949

Today I started to walk to the Riet Alp. There was lovely sunshine and I made my way down through the fields rejoicing in all the beauty. The fields were golden with the most beautiful kingcups and dandelions, and tiny gentians like blue gems were everywhere. The Brumbach and the Zillbach falls faced me. I walked rejoicing as though in heaven, awed

243

at the way all nature around me was sounding forth the utterances of God.

Ever since going through the Siege of Jerusalem in 1948 and being in constant danger of death, it seems that my physical senses have been quickened to enjoy the beauties, scents, and sounds of nature to a far higher degree than before. That is part of the legacy of joy and blessing which those terrifying experiences bestowed upon me.

In the old days when I visited Switzerland as a girl, I used to be thrilled by the beauties of nature in a special way: I loved the scent of the pine woods, of the damp cones and needles carpeting the ground; the sawn logs and moss- and lichen-covered rocks. But now it all means unutterably more to me. I find nature a book of marvels, the language of which I have just begun to understand and interpret. So I walked in ecstasy, with natural beauties around me speaking forth the praises and character of the Creator. Everything uttered his name.

I came to the sawmill beside the torrent which runs down the valley from the foot of the Brumbach falls. The water which I saw rushing so blithely over and among the rocks, and under the bridge, was the same water which, high over-head, had come to a great crisis and leaped so exultantly and with such blissful abandonment over the falls.

I stood on the bridge and looked at it. Yesterday I had asked myself, "What does the water do when, after its magnificent abandoned leap, it reaches the cruel rocks below, and there is no longer the ecstasy of leaping down, only a rough, rock-obstructed everyday course before it?"

On the bridge I saw, and laughed to see, what happens to the water. The bed of the torrent was strewn with huge rocks.

There were obstructions everywhere. But the water came rushing along, laughing and rejoicing and absolutely delighted to find its way over and around all the obstacles and difficulties. It seemed as happy and cheerful forcing its way among the grim rocks as when it threw itself down over the heights.

What a lesson I learned as I watched it: I think almost the loveliest of all of them. Day after day, once the leap of obedience has been made, the power of the waters following along behind, added to the steepness of the riverbed, makes the surmounting of difficulties and obstacles—of every kind—a daily delight. . . .

The Highest Place of All
. . . It is written:

> Let this mind be in you, which was also in Christ Jesus: who, being in the form of God, thought it not robbery to be equal with God; but made himself of no reputation, and took upon him the form of a servant, and was made in the likeness of men: and being found in fashion as a man, he humbled himself, and became obedient unto death, even the death of the cross. Wherefore God also hath highly exalted him, and given him a name which is above every name: that at the name of Jesus every knee should bow, of things in heaven, and things in earth, and things under the earth; and that every tongue should confess that Jesus Christ is Lord, to the glory of God the Father. That ye may be blameless and harmless, the sons of God, without rebuke, in the midst of a crooked and perverse nation, among whom ye shine

as lights in the world; holding forth the word of life
(Phil. 2:5-11, 15, 16).

Yes, from the highest place in the universe, the divine
Love leaped down to the lowest place of all. The little
Brumbach falls of the world are only tiny pictures and images
through which the Creator teaches us this staggering truth.
And Mont Blanc and the Alps are just a shadowy picture also
of the nature of eternal love. Oh! blest be the Creator,
because he himself shows us this awesome and glorious truth
through them: For he also longs to make us little true images
and reflectors of his divine love. . . .

[After returning to the Holy Land] I found myself entering
upon a completely new life of unexpected surprises and
challenges. I began my writing ministry, and then very soon,
started traveling from country to country around the world.

Six years later, in 1955, I was privileged just once more to
visit Braunwald, and there, sitting on the green slopes overlooking the Ortstock mountain, I wrote *Hinds' Feet on High
Places,* and so brought to birth in written form the messages
conceived in that same place six years earlier.

Oh, what a life of wonderful joy, adventure, and ever-
deepening love the Good Shepherd leads us all to! As we
follow him along the path of life, let us leave him to choose
every step of the way, as we live in his radiant presence and
are ever led to still higher places.

Glory be to him forever! Amen.

Bibliography

Bryers, Bessie. *To Them That Obey: An account of the development of the work of the Friends' Evangelistic Band.* Colchester, Essex, England: fellowship for Evangelising Britain's Villages, 1969.

Crombie, Kelvin J. *For the Love of Zion.* London: Hodder & Stoughton, 1991.

Hurnard, Hannah. *Eagles' Wings to Higher Places.* San Francisco: Harper & Row, 1983.

———. *God's Transmitters.* Wheaton, Ill.: Tyndale House Publishers, Inc., 1976.

———. *Hearing Heart.* Wheaton, Ill.: Tyndale House Publishers Inc., 1976.

———. *Hinds' Feet on High Places.* Wheaton, Ill.: Tyndale House Publishers, Inc., 1975.

———. *Kingdom of Love.* Wheaton, Ill.: Tyndale House Publishers, Inc., 1975.

———. *Lessons Learned on the Slopes of the High Places,* a pamphlet published in 1986; included in the Tyndale House edition of *Hinds' Feet* currently in print.

———. *Mountains of Spices.* Wheaton, Ill.: Tyndale House Publishers, Inc., 1977.

———. *Thou Shalt Remember.* San Francisco: Harper & Row, 1988.

———. *Walking Among the Unseen.* Wheaton, Ill.: Tyndale House Publishers, Inc., 1977.

———. *Watchmen on the Walls: A Diary from Jerusalem.* London: Church Missions to Jews, 1950. (out of print)

———. *Wayfarer in the Land.* Wheaton, Ill.: Tyndale House Publishers, Inc., 1973.

———. *Winged Life.* Wheaton, Ill.: Tyndale House Publishers, Inc., 1975.

Lewis, C. S. *The Great Divorce.* New York: Macmillan Publishing Co., 1946.

Discover these inspirational classics from Hannah Hurnard

GOD'S TRANSMITTERS 0-8423-1085-1
By practicing the principles of faith and love, we can serve God by becoming transmitters of his love through prayer.

HEARING HEART 0-8423-1405-9
This autobiographical account describes how God's transforming power replaced Hannah's despair and fear with his joy.

HINDS' FEET ON HIGH PLACES 0-8423-1429-6
Through dramatic allegory, this best-seller depicts the yearning of God's children to reach new heights of love and joy.

KINGDOM OF LOVE 0-8423-2080-6
Learn how to turn control of your mind and heart over to God and experience the glory and joy of his kingdom here on earth.

MOUNTAINS OF SPICES 0-8423-4611-2
This allegory compares the nine spices mentioned in Song of Solomon with the nine fruits of the Spirit.

WALKING AMONG THE UNSEEN 0-8423-7805-7
In leading readers to discover Christ's church at work in the spiritual world, Hurnard opens the door to spiritual joy.

WAYFARER IN THE LAND 0-8423-7823-5
The Lord's care and guidance are vividly demonstrated in this account of the author's missionary work in Israel.

WINGED LIFE 0-8423-8225-9
Experience a fulfilling Christian life by allowing God to transform your thoughts through attitudes of praise and pure thinking.